ANXIOUS CHRISTIANS

Kenneth Redgrave is in private practice as a psychotherapist (UKCP), and although his work is now mainly with adults he has had many years of specialist children's work. He has experienced a broad professional life, varying from church social work (Chester diocese) to university and further education lecturer in Human Growth and Behaviour, and at one time he was Deputy Children's Officer (Cambridgeshire). His early academic training included religious studies, philosophy and psychology (University of Durham). He is a member of a Bible-based Cheshire church.

Anxious Christians

Psychological Problems and Christian Faith

Kenneth Redgrave

Published in Great Britain in 2002
Society for Promoting Christian Knowledge
Holy Trinity Church
Marylebone Road
London NW1 4DU

British Library Cataloguing-in-Publication Data

A catalogue record for this book is available from the
British Library

ISBN 0–281–05507–6

1 3 5 7 9 10 8 6 4 2

Typeset by Trinity Typing, Wark-on-Tweed
Printed in Great Britain by Bookmarque Ltd, Croydon, Surrey

To my father,

the Revd H. H. Redgrave MA,

one time rector of Stow-Bedon

and Breckles, Norfolk

Contents

Acknowledgements   ix

ONE   1
    Introduction   1
    The unconscious and its function   3
    The learning process   5
    Learning by conditioning: classical and operant   8
    Guilt feelings and conflict   10
    The attachment process   12
    Psychology, psychiatry and all that!   17

TWO   22
    An inability to express feelings   22
    Having low self-esteem   27
    Eating distress   32
    Fears, phobias and panic attacks   46
    Relationship dynamics, and the influence of the
       premenstrual syndrome (PMS)   58

THREE   68
    Shyness and lack of confidence   69
    Compulsive obsessional thoughts   81
    Chronic anxiety and difficulties in decision-making   84
    Problems in controlling anger, and the search for
       meaning   91
    Stress, tension and irritable bowel syndrome
       (IBS)   99

FOUR   105
 Sensitive children   105
 Children who are made 'scapegoats'   109
 Mixed-up adolescents and over-strict parents   112
 Problems in integrating 'second families'   117
 Difficulties in being able to forgive a former
    partner   124
 Other physical conditions that affect our emotions   132
 Feeling condemned by God   136

FIVE   143
 What do we believe? What do we imagine?   143
 How do we feel? How do we respond?   148
 What pressures are we under? Where do we come
    from?   154
 Uncertainty   156
 Certainty   158
 Danger: unexploded bomb!   160
 'Comforting words' and 'scary words'   163
 Love   166

Appendix A: Psychotherapy and Counselling
    Organizations   173
Appendix B: Christian Counselling/Counsellors   175
References   177

Acknowledgements

I am grateful for all the advice and help I have received in the production of this book, and wish to express my thanks to Canon John Gunstone, and to the Revd C. G. Redgrave for reading the typescript and making suggestions for improvements. My thanks also to Alison Barr, Senior Editor, SPCK, to Linda Carroll for the copy-editing, to Kathryn Wolfendale, Project Editor, SPCK, and to Sarah Phillimore and Sheila Redgrave for their typing. I would like to acknowledge the Zondervan Publishing House and Philip Yancey for the quotations from the book *What's So Amazing About Grace?*, and also Human Givens Publishing for the extract from *The Therapist* journal.

In order to meet the objectives I had in mind when writing the book, I have drawn upon dozens of cases that were similar, but obviously never exactly the same. This means that the cases in the book represent persons and situations likely to be met anywhere in the modern world. While presenting a cross-section of psycho-social problems, none represents a particular individual or family I have treated in my practice.

One

And if the healing art is most divine, it must occupy itself with the soul as well as the body.

Apollonius of Tyana

Introduction

Why doesn't everyone who is a Christian feel happy? In fact, why do some people feel downright miserable, or even scared, when they are Christians? Wasn't Jesus Christ meant to take it all away – all that depression and those feelings of guilt and not being good enough. Wasn't it all meant to evaporate the day you became a Christian?

Some people would say your faith is too weak, or you haven't prayed hard enough. But what if your faith is very strong, and you spend hours in prayer, and you read the lessons in church, and so on? It doesn't seem fair that someone who should then come along, someone who maybe says they are led by the Lord, and just announce that you haven't enough faith. And suppose you just cannot understand the answers to some profound question like 'Why suffering?', and someone says that if you had enough faith you wouldn't ask such questions. That's what happened to poor old Job. He kept asking such questions – just couldn't get them out of his mind. I can imagine what some modern clever people would say to him. They'd say, 'You've got an obsession, Job', or if they were very intellectual they might give him a book (sixth edition) entitled something like *The Metaphysical and Transcendental Aspects of Human Dysfunction, associated with Physical or Psychic Distress*! And Job would be none the wiser.

So what is it that bugs so many people, even Christians, today? But before we dive into an answer of that question, which is a very big one, let's ask about the sort of suffering that people experience. I have used the word 'suffering', but I am not writing mainly about physical suffering. How is it that when you've got 'everything' – good health, good job, friends, family, etc. – one scary feeling after another looms up, making you feel trapped in a sort of 'mind' or 'spiritual' pit? You're supposed to be forgiven, aren't you? How is it that you can't forgive yourself? Why do people keep dredging up things to feel guilty about when another part of themselves says 'that's ridiculous', and why does it go on when they prayed for forgiveness? Don't tell me – this is where we came in: 'You haven't got enough faith!' This is not true, though we are talking about people who have faith, who pray, and yet are still unhappy.

In this book I want to share a journey of discovery with you. Partly I want to look at how we are made, and partly I want to look at how our creator wants us to relate to one another, and this includes the way that parents relate to their children. A lot of Christians are scared to look within; scared of discovering things about themselves. Whole church groups are sometimes scared by new ideas, and some people very quickly see a threat in any new approach, just as our ancestors did when people believed the sun went round the earth! There was a time, for instance, when psychology was definitely seen as a threat – if not the actual work of the devil. But nowadays it is taught alongside pastoral theology in theological colleges. Which is not to say that all ideas of all psychologists should be embraced by us, any more than all ideas of all theologians should be.

I hope to show that much of our unhappiness, anxiety, and irrational feelings of guilt are the result of human disregard for right psychological approaches, and furthermore, that this disregard for right psychological approaches to life, especially to other people in our lives, goes directly against the teachings of our Lord Jesus Christ.

Some Christians worry about any explanation of human behaviour because they feel it might do away with the concept of sin, or it might absolve people from personal blame. At the end of this book 'sin' will still be there, and so will 'personal responsibility', but the reader's concept of sin may have broadened rather than diminished.

But, you may say, what is there to find out about myself? Apart from the first few years of life, I am well aware of everything that has ever happened to me, both nice and nasty, and surely those very early months and years don't count for much anyway? You may continue by pointing out that you have a good memory, that you know where you came from, and – hopefully – where you are going.

But don't be so sure that you are aware of everything that has ever happened to you, even things that occurred after you first started school. As this book unfolds I hope you will be able to accept that, at least in this life, we cope much better (usually) by carrying around a lot of knowledge of which we are aware ('conscious of') and a lot more 'knowledge' of which we are unaware. So some of this 'unconscious' stuff is only temporarily put on one side, forgotten, ignored, but we can recall it when we need it. Great, marvellous! God thought it out long before we invented computers with memory banks!

The unconscious and its function

Many Christian counsellors and psychologists accept that we all have useful 'memory banks', and that some of our experiences may at times be 'stored' so deeply that we cannot retrieve them, but they do not place as much emphasis on the so-called unconscious part of the mind as many secular psychologists do. As a Christian therapist, I feel that our understanding of human psychology must rest upon certain biblical principles or boundaries, which are these:

- Humans are created beings (i.e. created by God).
- Humans are divine image-bearers (and therefore distinguished from all other life forms).
- Humans are both physical and spiritual (i.e. they are both material and immaterial).

(Shields and Bredfeldt, 2001)

It is important that readers should know this because, although I shall be often drawing upon ideas of psychology and even Freud's so-called psychoanalysis, I do not have to accept all the theories (or hypotheses) in an uncritical way. However, by spelling out these basic boundaries now, it will spare me having to go into all the pros and cons every time I draw upon a psychological concept. I hope, therefore, that readers will be able to accept the proposition that we have part of ourselves that is open and conscious, and a part of ourselves that functions in what we call the unconscious. It seems, in fact, that we are capable of locking away some of our experiences – not just forgetting them, but totally blocking them out. And usually we are not even aware that we are doing this. As Christians, we can see this as a God-given, God-designed ability.

Nevertheless, because of the lives we live, and the societies we have created, this 'blocking out' can work in a harmful way. It can also function in a way that 'works' for the time being but comes 'unstuck' later on. I have worked with children who, as children, 'forgot' (or repressed the memory) that their parents had rejected them and put them in the care of others. They needed to 'see' their parents as good, caring and responsible. Later, however, as young adults, their hidden anger towards the parents broke through into consciousness, often not without a struggle, and those young people had to be helped. But the unconscious – the 'kidding themselves', that went on in childhood – protected them to some extent when they were young. That of course is all very sad, but readers will discover other examples of unconscious elements in the case histories that are given in the following chapters.

Above I have used the word 'repressed', but we have to remember that most of the time *repression* is a normal process. When the usual hardships of life, and difficulties of interaction and of growing up, come and slap us down, we often success- fully repress these memories and so are able to cope adequately with life. We are made in such a way as to be able to carry lots of stored information – information remains stored and does us no harm. We have, and need, an unconscious as well as a conscious mind.

Psychologists are aware of this clever act of repression, and understand that it is a means of defence. Therefore they call it a *defence mechanism*. The term is a bit harsh because it somewhat reminds us of machines, and we know that we are not just pieces of mechanical equipment. Defence mechanisms, though, are important means of protecting our inner beings – and there are various examples of defence mechanisms in the case histories that follow.

The learning process

Let's look at some other important ways in which we are made and, more to the point, ways in which we function. You may think it a commonplace, and not a very profound statement, if we say we are made with an ability to learn. But hold on, what psychologists call the 'learning process' also turns out to have a lot to do with anxiety and FEAR. I have put the word 'fear' in capitals. Why? Because I feel it is one of the most crippling feelings we humans can experience.

Here are some lines from a rather old-fashioned hymn, but read them carefully:

> How sweet the name of Jesus sounds
> In a believer's ear!
> It soothes his sorrows, heals his wounds
> And drives away his *fear* (my italics).

But does Jesus drive away fear? Can he, will he, drive away fear? I, and many other Christians, happen to believe that he can and does. However, we also believe that on account of the mess that humanity – especially twentieth- and twenty-first-century Western humanity – is making of life, we may often be directed by God to make use of knowledge and healing processes that go beyond merely singing in the 'name' of Jesus.

There can be little doubt in the mind of the Christian that, despite the indications to the effect that we may have to suffer hardship, and even agony, our Lord did not want us to be suffering intense, chronic anxiety, and fear is always somewhere around with anxiety. Did he not say: 'And so I tell you not to worry about the food you need to stay alive, or about the clothes you need for your body. Life is much more important than food, and the body much more important than clothes' (Luke 12.22–3, GNB)? And didn't his great messenger, Paul, tell the Philippians: 'Do not be anxious about anything, but in everything, by prayer and petition, with thanksgiving, present your requests to God. And the peace of God, which transcends all understanding, will guard your hearts and your minds in Christ Jesus' (Philippians 4.6–7)?

So does all this mean that God condemns us if we ever experience fear? Or if we experience anxiety? Of course not. If we think like that we are forgetting a very important central theme of the Christian message, which is that Jesus was not only divine but also fully human. This may seem a difficult paradox to grasp at first, but we have to remember that he felt temptation and sadness, became angry, and certainly experienced anxiety and fear: 'In great anguish he prayed even more fervently; his sweat was like drops of blood falling to the ground' (Luke 22.44, GNB).

Jesus must have known how hard it is to eliminate some forms of anxiety and fear. When he spoke about not worrying about food and clothes, he wasn't addressing starving people or even those who were poverty-stricken. Bear in mind that he was concerned even when a great crowd followed him and had walked miles in the heat to listen to him. He was concerned about their physical need for food, but he was also more than concerned ('filled with pity', GNB) over their spiritual state.

When Jesus is talking about food and clothes, he is saying something profound about the kind of society, the value system, the anxiety-ridden states that people can reach when they – that is whole societies – move away from the values their creator intends them to hold. Here is an extract from a modern journal, which in fact has a secular approach:

Our mental processes evolved to deal with a more primitive world than the crowded technological one we've created, and we are failing to comprehend, and adapt to modern life. Increasingly people are unsettled and afraid.

Therapists, doctors, counsellors, teachers, police and care workers of all kinds, can sense the pressure growing. They find themselves faced with a population whose members largely avoid facing up to their fear. The fear, of course, is kept in check somewhat by our perennial, almost frenzied, search for emotional stimulation and entertainment, which we use to distract ourselves from confronting its cause. But even though we're surrounded by distractions, the incidence of psychiatric disorders is on the increase. Daily more people sink into apathy, depression, illness, depravity, criminality and violence. (*The Therapist*, 1993)

Don't become a society or an individual where the highest values are attached to personal power, personal ownership of 'the best'. (What is the best anyway?) This is the message of Luke 12.22–3 quoted above.

Jesus' message, his guidance, is as valid today as on the day he spoke it: don't make personal power and success your main aim in life. Don't make a bigger this, or an updated that ('in case I look out of date'), our objective in life. This is not a plea for poverty, nor is it a statement against ownership. It is a statement that says, for your own sake, for your good health, for your fulfilment, for your becoming a more relaxed society or individual, remember the other values of love, care, art, music, talking and singing – and, above all, remember those deeper, richer spiritual needs of life. Jesus said, `Life is much more important than food and the body much more important than clothes' (although, of course, Jesus well knew that people needed both food and clothes).

Learning by conditioning: classical and operant

Right from the start, students of psychology will read about two basic forms of learning. I have no intention of turning this book into a textbook on psychology, but we need to remind ourselves that human organisms have a propensity, of which they may be unaware, to respond in a set manner to certain stimuli – something happening outside themselves, for example. Without our being aware of them, all sorts of glandular reactions may occur in reaction to events – for example, reactions designed to save a person from imminent danger. Most people know that in the face of something terrifying, or just scary, the body releases adrenaline (epinephrine) and other hormones into the bloodstream. In fact, something like 30 hormones may be released, each playing a role in the body's adjustment to 'emergency' situations. All this is just a glimpse at the wonderful design of our physical nature. But most of these reactions of the body are *automatic*, a conditioned reflex. This is known as *classical conditioning*.

Although we are not aware of the release of all these separate hormones in situations of acute stress, we are aware of changes in our body function – such as an increased heart rate, dry mouth and tremors; and others watching us may notice that our pupils have become dilated ('wide-eyed'). Young children, of course, may even wet themselves. But all this is a part of our 'fight or flight' readiness. We may, in the face of danger, run very fast (because of the hormones and sugar released) or fight the 'monster' (again with the extra energy released).

So this can all be very useful, and is God-designed. But imagine now that we misuse God's gift and decide to torture people. Suppose we torture people who up to now have loved the ordinary things in life, including the sounds of birds singing. Imagine that whenever they are tortured the sound of birds singing is played over on a tape. What would happen to our victims? They would find that even after being rescued, for a long time – perhaps indefinitely without treatment – all the symptoms of cold fear would emerge as soon as they heard the bird-song. This would be an example of classical conditioning. Their bodies have 'learnt' to react in this way even though they know that they are now safe.

We are meant to be able to learn. When we learn to perform the multitudinous actions we do hour by hour, we become so much more efficient, and we become unconscious of the details. We learnt to walk, to balance, etc., as infants. Now as adults we just walk, just balance. Think how problematic life would be if we had to relearn every time we stood up!

Much of our learning, however, is more complex than classical conditioning. A great deal of our learning uses what psychologists call *operant conditioning*, which again depends very much on 'reward' (emotional at times) and 'punishment' (again, this may be only emotional). Perhaps instead we might use the terms 'satisfying' and 'non-satisfying', which are not so strong as 'reward' and 'punishment'.

So as children we learn to behave in a socialized way, not because our parents consistently beat us up (even though some do), but because as we become adults we feel it is rewarding or satisfying to be accepted, to be approved of. Approval is very satisfying. Approval is reward. If I open a door and invite my friend to go through first I can say (in psychology jargon) I have performed an *operant*. It was not an automatic response, but a learnt response – operant conditioning.

And now comes the crunch. From day one of our lives, and some would even say pre-birth, we are forced to respond in one way or another to the events surrounding us, and especially to the influence of people caring for us. As children, we make use of this learning process in order to make sense of the world, but very soon we may meet with intense pressures and conflicts – which are probably not even noticed by the adults in our lives. In order to cope with these conflicts and pressures (which produce emotional reactions), we 'adjust' to them, which is 'helpful' in the short term. It sort of protects the 'inner child'. And, in any case, people bigger than us have more power and we have a built-in tendency to copy whenever we can.

Much of this adjusting and coping, however, may turn out to be very damaging to the child's developing personality, and this is especially so where parents or other care-givers are themselves poorly adjusted to life. Thus the child learns to respond in ways that seem to avoid conflict, or to avoid dealing with conflict, and gradually a behavioural and belief system is developed.

Recently one female client said to me, 'My mother taught me to hate men'. Yet this woman had already been married twice and now lived unhappily with her third husband. Although she now, as an adult, could disagree with her mother's views she was unable to lose certain rejecting feelings connected with the sexual act. We can also develop prejudices, preconceived ideas about people or institutions, as a result of the learning process. In some societies Christians have been brought up to view all Jews as wicked. Some children are still taught that boys (i.e. all boys) must be tough, and not cry, and not do such 'girlish' things as write poetry or knit. Many little boys who are natural poets and are artistic suffer a lot of stress because of such teaching.

Guilt feelings and conflict

Some people come to therapists such as myself for help with marital problems. As children somewhere along the line they 'learnt' that all sex is nasty. Some have learnt to hide their true selves, even from themselves. For example, many Christians feel a deep sense of frustration because they always pretend that they never get angry. Part of their belief system is that anger itself is bad. But there's another, hidden, subtle part of their belief system, which is telling them that to be angry is to let down . . . God? In fact, it may not be God, although they may interpret it that way. Unconsciously, and sometimes consciously, they feel they are betraying Mother or Father, or someone else who exercised influence (or power) in their upbringing. All sorts of influences have taught us, especially as children, that we are bad or wicked if we think about our parents negatively. Does it not say in the Bible, 'Honour your father and mother' (Exodus 20.12)? Yes it does, and in some modern versions this may be translated 'Respect your father and mother'. And as adults we can do just that: honour or respect (treat as we would any human being), but also not be blind to their shortcomings.

Many people, though, are surrounded by feelings of guilt when it comes to acknowledging that their parents were not perfect, and some experience terrible tension as a result of the way they were pinned down emotionally. I can think of one 14-year-old girl who was a frequent truant from school. She lived alone with her father whose intolerable behaviour had driven her mother into a psychiatric hospital. This girl was under enormous emotional stress. She was being given a 'double bind message' (two conflicting messages at once) from her father. She felt dutiful towards both her parents, yet she did not now want to lose her father as well as her mother.

The 'double bind message' her father gave her was, 'You should be at school – you'll get me into trouble if you don't go.' But also, 'I'm depressed, it's your mother's fault, I'm lonely. One of these evenings you'll come home and find my body on the floor!' Then he'd swish his finger across his throat to indicate suicide. I'm sure that 'Honour your father . . .' did not mean for this child, 'Pretend your dad is perfect, all-loving and very nice', but that is the picture many children cling to while at the same time experiencing great inner conflict.

Some children learn that only clever, angelic or 'successful' children (maybe like their brother or sister) are acceptable. Perhaps they feel that they are only loved and valued if they are beautiful. Such children can grow up completely lacking in self-esteem. Worse, as a result of all this learning, they may develop a stammer, put on weight, or become vicious. They may learn that they are 'hopeless', 'unacceptable', even 'un-lovable' – all of which of course are untrue.

Hopefully, enough has been said here to make it clear that although God gave us the potential and ability to learn, this process can malfunction. It can become part of humanity's pain. It may become mingled with sin.

The attachment process

The attachment process is another fascinating aspect of human behaviour; it highlights a need, a developmental need. At first mention, this behaviour or process may seem commonplace, almost overlooked even in books on psychology, yet if it goes wrong the results can be devastating.

I am not using the term 'attachment' here as a loose term expressing a sentimental mood or attitude – the way it is used when we refer to being attached to (i.e. 'fond of') a particular model of car or a holiday destination. I am not using it even in the stronger sense of being attached to a group of friends – 'buddies' or 'mates'.

In the animal kingdom there is a process called *imprinting*, which works to protect the infant animal. The naturalist Konrad Lorenz did a lot of work on imprinting and he showed that newly hatched geese, for example, will become 'imprinted' by the first moving object in their lives, which of course in most cases will be the female parent. Imprinting seems to create, or 'imprint', an impression in the infant animal's brain that causes it to follow and keep close to the 'imprinter'. In the case of newly hatched geese, it is quite easy for a human being to act as the imprinter, in which case all the little newly hatched chicks or goslings will follow the human just as if she or he were their real parent. There are pictures of Lorenz crossing a busy street with a string of goslings following him!

Chicks of all sorts can become imprinted, even by a coloured balloon. Of course the balloon won't actually protect the chicks in the natural state, but because they have an instinct to get up and go soon after they are hatched, they will follow regardless.

Attachment in human beings is a rather more complex process, and its proper development depends not so much on the physical aspects of the environment, but on the successful emotional development of the person through childhood as he or she receives emotional stimulation from parents and siblings. In fact, some experts claim that much of our mental and social life as adults is affected by the attachment experiences of our childhood.

Where 'good-enough attachment' develops in a child towards adults (usually parents and siblings), we can say that the child develops a sense of 'safe belongingness'. You may be surprised to learn that this sense of safe belongingness does not depend all that much on the physical care the child receives, but on something far more subtle. A child may, for example, be fed by a particular adult (and it used to be thought that the feeding developed the attachment), but he or she will attach to whoever is able to give the emotional warmth and the proper emotionally attached physical holding/cuddling. In what is called 'good-enough parenting', the feeders and the providers of emotional satisfaction are the natural parents.

However, in early infancy, or even with the newly born, 'messages' are received by the infant from those caring for them, and the baby can begin to develop all sorts of emotional responses that affect the attachment process and ultimately the personality. Here is one example from my own experience as a therapist. It concerns a newborn baby who was placed straight from hospital (at about ten days old) into the care of a new short-term (pre-adoptive) foster mother.

This foster mother was a 'good-enough parent' in her own right and had two happy and normal young children of about six and eight years old. She had never before cared for a newborn baby whom she knew would be parted from her after about eight weeks when the baby would be placed with permanent adopters. The foster mother had a terrible time with the baby who cried and cried. Health visitors and doctors described him as an 'irritable' baby. The child began to look quite poorly, but nothing physically wrong could be found.

Because the new foster mother felt she could not go on, and her own children were suffering as a result of her tiredness, the baby was moved, after only two weeks, into the permanent adopters' home. The adopters had been warned that they were likely to have a tiring time, with an 'irritable' baby. Yet within

24 hours the baby settled down and from then on was no more trouble than the average 'good baby' (a shocking term!).

The original foster mother, who experienced all the trouble, never took on any more babies. She told me that, looking back, she could see that she had *looked after* the baby, but that all the time she had felt a terrible pain, 'sort of in my heart or soul', and that she had tried hard 'not to let myself get to love the baby. I used to make sure I didn't hold him too close to me and all that kind of thing . . .' No doubt we were dealing with a particularly sensitive baby and foster mother in this case, but even though nine months is said to be the time when attachment has formed in human babies, this child was already picking up signals, and was in fact missing something – and perhaps even becoming angry inside himself. He was created to be loved, but being loved was being denied to him.

Vera Fahlberg, the American paediatrician and psychotherapist, has given the following list of personal growth accomplishments that are helped by 'good-enough attachment'. A strong attachment can enable a child to:

- Attain his/her full intellectual potential.
- Sort out what he/she perceives.
- Think logically.
- Develop social emotions.
- Trust others.
- Develop a conscience.
- Become self-reliant.
- Cope better with stress and frustration.
- Reduce feelings of jealousy.
- Overcome common fears and worries.
- Increase feelings of self-worth.

(Fahlberg, 1991)

You will see from this list the extent to which the attachment process affects the development of the personality.

Dr John Bowlby has been one of the main researchers and writers concerning attachment. He has stated:

What for convenience I am terming attachment theory is a way of conceptualising the propensity of human beings to make strong affectional bonds to particular others and of explaining the many forms of emotional distress and personality disturbance, including anxiety, anger, depression, and emotional detachment . . . Advocates of attachment theory argue that many forms of psychiatric disturbance can be attributed either to deviations in the development of attachment behaviour or, more rarely, to failure of its development; and also that the theory casts light on both the origin and treatment of these conditions. (Bowlby, 1986)

So we are not dealing here, as I said above, with just a slushy 'Oh, how adorable!' sentiment. We are dealing with an aspect of development that is vital for human emotional and general mental health. For many years I have worked with children and young people who have been rejected, cast out, or moved from one 'carer' to another. These are children who could not attach, and who began to develop a protective 'emotional skin' to stop people attaching to them because they had already been hurt too much. These youngsters often developed into aggressive, law-breaking, unhappy, drug-taking adults.

These are the more extreme examples of the effects of poor attachment experiences, but it is important to remember that many of us may be negatively affected in less extreme ways as a result of the quality of nurture we received, and the extent to which we missed out on warmth, closeness, being held, being valued. Valued not on account of our achievements or looks, but just because we existed in the lives of our caregivers. Some of us may not have had these and other important needs met.

It seems, despite the fact that I could quote many scientific papers on 'attachment', that although we may not equate attachment with love, yet in 'good-enough attachment' and bonding there must be elements that are of the quality of love, of caring love. This brings us back to the amazing purpose and design of God, and his intentions. Clearly, attachment devoid of *love* (however much philosophers may wish to argue over that word) won't work. We are designed, if you like, to be brought up in love. Love is essential to our mental health – ultimately there is a deep spiritual content required for our proper fulfilment.

But, alas, even with 'love' and attachment so much can go wrong. In fact, love, or what passes for it, is often used to 'blackmail' a child – and even adult offspring. In other words, parents find ways of controlling their offspring by emotional blackmail. Think of the married woman whose mother still dominates her life, by verbally punishing her for the way she's running her home or bringing up her children. Why can't the married woman tell her mother to 'get lost', so to speak? It is because, when she was a child, Mum dominated her to the extent that she would now feel intolerably guilty were she to stand up for herself. And, in any case, her mother might use another 'weapon': she'd cut her off, sulk, not speak or communicate with her, put the phone down if she rang to apologize. This mother would probably call her behaviour 'affection'! And people might even comment how 'attached' she is to her daughter, and vice versa. However, in reality this does not represent 'good-enough attachment'. It might actually represent anxious attachment, which some children display even to parents who have abused them.

Here we have looked briefly at just a few of the important psychological processes that form part of human behaviour. These processes are not in themselves examples of neuroses, but of normal mental functioning of human beings. Our creator wanted us to be learning (and intelligent) individuals, and he designed the marvellous process of attachment with its involvement of care-giving love. But God also saw to it that under certain degrees of stress we should be able to block out, repress, and to assign to the unconscious certain experiences.

But these same processes, and many more, may be misused to injure or entrap others in the most subtle of ways, and they may also be misused to entrap, or even lose, part of the self.

They may be misused by the individual to develop deep unconscious pressures of guilt where no guilt exists in the eyes of God, or to create intense anxiety within the self even to the extent of damaging the physical functioning of the body. Even our immune systems may be adversely affected by prolonged anxiety or depression.

Psychology, psychiatry and all that!

Some Christian leaders warmly embrace psychology, whereas others would have us believe that all psychology, or all 'alternative medicine', is the work of the devil. Some of those leaders who do embrace it even become psychotherapists or counsellors. (Mind you, it is hard to imagine any minister with a pastoral mission who is not in reality also a counsellor.)

Slowly, the overall mood is changing. There is a growing acceptance that psychology and the sciences and arts, which have developed from it, have a contribution to make in the spiritual as well as the medical and social fields. And the names of certain Christian writers who are psychiatrists or psychotherapists have become household names in some Christian communities and families.

Many of you will be familiar with the name of Dr James Dobson. James is a psychologist and family counsellor, who has helped many Christian families cope adequately with child-rearing, marriage, sexuality, homemaking and teenagers. Others will be familiar with the name of Dr Paul Tournier, a medical doctor who has written, 'Our profession is a priestly ministry. I should like to see the church consecrate doctors just as it ordains ministers. This would be in conformity with the gospel.'

More recently, William West, lecturer in counselling studies at the University of Manchester, has stated that unless the 'spiritual dimension' is included, psychotherapy 'will not fulfil its potential role, and the healing that is necessary is likely to be limited and incomplete' (West, 2000). Dr Harry Shields and Dr Gary Bredfeldt, both pastoral counsellors and professors, wrote a book called *Caring for Souls*. These expert therapists write, 'It goes without saying that those who help others will want to spend time in regular study of and meditation on the Word of God. They will also spend time in prayer for themselves and those they serve' (Shields and Bredfeldt, 2001).

Many Christian counsellors and psychotherapists also contribute articles to Christian journals, and many Christian ministers are trained counsellors. There are in fact Christian journals specializing in the convergence of body, mind and spirit. However, some Christian ministers still have doubts about psychological theories and practices, and these matters are dealt with more fully in Chapter Five.

I have said almost enough on this point. Attempting to understand human psychology and to use it to the benefit of those who are burdened with anxiety should be at least as acceptable as attempting to understand how the various chemical changes in the body adversely affect people, and how dispensing drugs may help sufferers. Both may be abused, but both – if used properly – may be accepted as gifts from God. So now let's describe how the various therapists differ and what they offer.

The cartoon picture of a *psychiatrist* is of a doctor seated beside, or slightly behind, his patient who lies on a bed or chaise-longue. The doctor, usually pictured as a slightly eccentric 'professor' type, has his notepad in hand and his pen at the alert, and awaits the profundities that he expects to issue from the depths of his patient's unconscious.

This picture has come down from the accounts we have received concerning the practice of such father figures of psychiatry as Sigmund Freud and Carl Jung. In fact, what they practised would today be described as psychotherapy rather than psychiatry.

Patients visiting a psychiatrist today would probably find him or her seated behind a desk. A psychiatrist has to be a doctor – that is to say, a medically qualified person. She or he will, however, have taken further training specifically concerned with psychological ill health. But the other big difference between the real modern psychiatrist and the cartoon picture lies in the fact that modern psychiatrists, by and large, practise drug therapy treatment, along with other physical, even surgical treatments. These include the use of electroconvulsive therapy (ECT). Patients, though, will often find that they are referred for so-called 'talk therapy' to a psychologist or a psychotherapist who may be team members working alongside the consultant psychiatrist.

Now consider the term *psychologist*. Most psychologists will not be medical doctors, but if they are registered and 'chartered' they will have been well and rigorously trained, and some of them will be seen as vital elements in any mental health team. But the term 'psychologist' is really what we call a 'generic' term. Only some of them have specialized in mental health (or ill health) problems; others have nothing to do with illness or anxiety or depression (at least, those are not their main professional concerns).

There are industrial psychologists, educational psychologists, social psychologists, experimental psychologists, sports psychologists, and even archaeological psychologists. So, because someone says he or she has a degree in psychology, it does not mean that they are qualified to treat people who suffer from anxiety, depression, or any other of the conditions we outline in this book.

However, I have left out the term *clinical psychologists* from the list given above. It is the clinical psychologist, in fact, who is qualified to treat people who are experiencing emotional upheaval, anxiety or depression, or suffering from various phobias. There are, though, fewer freelance clinical psychologists than there are freelance psychotherapists. Many clinical psychologists actually work as part of a clinical team in a hospital or other medical establishment. There are of course *child psychologists* too, who are concerned with the mental health of children.

So we now come to the *psychotherapists*. Like psychologists, most of these people are not medical doctors, although in fact some are – especially in the United States. Also, once again, the psychotherapists who are registered with recognized or 'accredited' professional bodies will not only have an examined and rigorous training behind them but, as with psychologists, will be bound by a 'code of professional conduct' which, if broken, will attract disciplinary action, punishment or even being struck off the register.

All psychotherapists (unlike some psychologists) are concerned with the treatment of psychological stress. Some of them, perhaps most, are 'general' practitioners in the sense that they will see patients (or some would say 'clients') from a broad span of psycho-social problems, such as I describe in the following chapters. Most have areas of specialization, so that, for instance, a psychotherapist taking a general or mixed group of clients may nevertheless be especially interested in (and have taken further training in) certain areas – perhaps eating disorders such as anorexia nervosa.

With regard to the national accredited registering bodies for psychologists, psychotherapists and counsellors, the main ones are given in Appendix A. But we need to be aware that in some countries at present, including Britain, anyone may advertise their services as either a counsellor or a psychotherapist regardless of how much they lack training or supervision, so it is very important to check on the qualifications professed and held by therapists, counsellors, psychotherapists and others. (See Appendix B for some guidance concerning Christian counsellors.) However, it is likely that a form of general registration will soon be required in Europe, as it is in the United States.

In the following chapters I shall look more closely at stress, anxiety and personal interaction, and how God wants us to live. I shall be introducing actual case histories, and looking at what these people said when they first came for help. Therapists call such statements the 'presenting problems'. Readers will be interested in the 'extended problems' that the presenting problems were often hiding.

In the case histories, no 'live case' will be recognized – except where I have been given permission by that client to report his actual problems. Usually, the case histories represent a mixture of recurring problems. To further protect confidentiality, I have changed ages and sibling and family groupings as well as the gender of individuals. However, because the problems themselves are so common, many readers whom I have never met will 'recognize' themselves in the book.

Two

Take from our lives the strain and stress.

In this and the following two chapters, our discussion will range around the problems presented by clients using psychotherapy. However, the cases I shall look at here are typical of any psychotherapy or counselling practice. The only difference is that rather more of this selection includes religious or faith matters.

You will see that quite often the so-called presenting problem is only part of the problem. Sometimes it is equivalent to the tip of the proverbial iceberg. So in each case I shall give a few sentences from the clients' own statements, and then I'll discuss and expand on these problems.

An inability to express feelings

Erica's presenting problem

'I was brought up to be a good, church-going, respectable citizen, a *proper* sort of person. Why is it that I find it almost impossible to ever express any kind of affection verbally? I am just 19 and I realize that in our family no one ever said anything tender ("soft" was the word we would have used). Has this affected me?'

Strange, isn't it, how in some families and some communities you can feel quite embarrassed by any expression of affection. Erica emphasizes the fact that she finds it almost impossible to express affection in words. However, some readers may have experienced difficulty in any show of affection. Yet we are writing about a phenomenon that is probably far more extensive among the so-called middle class or better off in our Western world than in other cultures.

Erica also asks, 'Has this affected me?' My own experience as a psychotherapist leads me to answer the question in a general way, and I would say that many adults are now finding that there is just something, something terribly important, that is missing from their childhood and adult completeness. I have even heard this described in terms of a gap or a hole. People have said that because they never experienced love, and have no memory of a parent ever having said 'I love you', they feel a sort of hole 'within'. They may put their hand on their breast and say 'It's up here I feel it – a sort of hole – something missing. If only my dad had *said* he loved me.' [Some say, 'If only Mum [or Dad] had said she [he] was proud of me.']

Some people actually go on trying to activate an expression of affection or approval from their parents. They spend the greater part of their lives trying to achieve some goal in order to hear Mum or Dad (or both) say 'I love you', or 'I'm proud of you'. But of course love should not depend upon the achievements of the loved person. In my book that is called *conditional love*. But the really sad thing is that this behaviour is very often found among people who actually *do* love, and may actually find their children a joy, but who cannot express it, and certainly not in words.

In some places, and this goes for the United States as well as Britain, the culture of the society inhibits fathers in particular from expressing loving sentiments. This is often accompanied by the myth that 'men don't feel'. The truth is that society has often dictated that if you are a 'real man' you will not express caring feelings, and you should also worry about your manhood if you feel these sentiments to any degree. This view is often projected into the hero types of popular television series and films, who take on the characteristics of automatons. Margo Maine, in her book called *Father Hunger*, says: 'One of the damaging effects of constricted communication between father and daughters is that even basic messages of acceptance are absent. The result is that daughters grow up wondering how dad feels about them, but they have no way of knowing since they never receive any feedback. They are quick to conclude that they have not "measured up" in some basic ways. They are desperate to please, but don't know how' (Maine, 1993).

Of course, it is not only daughters who suffer in this way, important though it is for the girl to have a positive fathering experience. Sons also suffer. The American television personality Oprah Winfrey interviewed several sets of three generations of men on one of her shows. These were grandfathers, fathers and sons. The middle generation, whom I am calling fathers, all suffered on account of their fathers never having expressed their love and appreciation. Some of them said that they strove even during their adulthood to achieve something, maybe 'status', maybe coming back to visit Dad having 'made it' in some job, but arriving in a Cadillac just to hear Dad say, 'I'm proud of you.'

Sadly, although they did in some cases hear those words, it came too late. It didn't mean anything by then. They explained the feeling as a 'hole', something missing. Several of them started out as fathers doing the same to their sons, whom Oprah also interviewed. Because the model of fathering they had received did not include the expression of feeling – or at least a verbal expression of feeling – towards their sons, they found it difficult to deviate from the model – embarrassing, unmanly!

Here's an extract from Jill Tweedie's autobiography, a section relating to her childhood. She had just discovered her essay had won a prize in a national competition, and her school magazine had printed a notice about it. She'd told her mother and they were waiting to tell the good news to her father. But he marched in from work, fed up with the world and with the 'idiots' in his department:

> 'Oh, dear,' said Mother. 'Well we've got some good news, anyway.' She bobbed her head at me and, glowing, I stepped forward.
> 'I won a prize,' I said. 'For essays. It's printed here. Mummy's read it. She thinks it's good.'

'What your mother knows about essays," said the Cleft [her father] heavily, 'could be written on the head of one of her dressmaking pins.'

'Alistair!' said Mother, reproachful.

'As for you, young lady. Fine, you've won a prize. Just don't go thinking what you win at school has anything to do with the real world out there. You think you're clever? Let me tell you, you haven't half the brains, never will have so don't give yourself airs. And I'll tell you something else. It's not cleverness that counts; it's hard work, and character. Without them you'll end up no more than a smart Alec, and you're well down that road already.' (Tweedie, 1993)

It seems that Jill Tweedie was constantly given the message from her father that she was unintelligent, unattractive, and unlike himself in every way. Even if it were true that school prizes were no guarantee of success in the adult world this was not the time to ram it home. Judging from her autobiography, the message from her father seemed to be 'You have no right to exist.'

But what about Jill Tweedie's father's own experience of being parented? What about the model those Oprah Winfrey grandfathers had from their fathers? So far as we know, all these parents were good, and probably even 'God-fearing' citizens and parents, but they had received as a part of the world's wisdom or custom that it is best, or proper, to behave towards one's children in a way that almost denied any feelings of affection, of belongingness.

Lots of people find it very hard to allow the natural part of themselves to speak out, that part that expresses warmth, affection, belongingness, nearness, love, and to express it verbally, 'I love you'. No, that's getting emotional, we mustn't be emotional! But worse, many people experience that 'hole' somewhere deep inside themselves. But should the 'hole' still be there when you are a Christian, when God has taken you into his care? And then what about those feelings of guilt: 'I shouldn't feel a "hole" inside because I have Christ – Christ within me, Christ above me', etc.

But remember what I have already said concerning the God-given power of humans to learn, and also the God-ordained scheme of loving, caring and parenting that every child should have experienced. The person who experiences a 'hole', feels unable to express feelings of love that are trapped within, is possibly carrying psychological scars or wounds.

Even those of us who were brought up in 'good' respect-able families have probably experienced incompleteness be-cause our society, or culture, or individual care-giver did not convey feelings of love, care and value. That can be termed sinful. Sin is not to be seen only in dark schemes, plotting, lying and stealing. Sin is also that which goes against God's designs and, we could say, God's nature. Your parents or care-givers might unconsciously, even while desiring your welfare, have been 'in sin', simply because they failed to live in God's design. This does not mean that they were 'bad' people, but if you have missed out on parental love, and cannot express your own feelings of love, then you have missed out on something God intended you to have.

But you can be helped. Counselling and psychotherapy in the right hands is as much a God-given healing process as the medical skills we so often pray that our doctors may have. Of course there are people whose empty feelings disappeared as soon as Christ came into their lives, just as there are people who have been healed physically as a result of God's miracu-lous intervention. But the miracle, or spontaneous change in feelings, is not the only way that God works. He works through doctors and other physical healers, and he also works through pastors, counsellors, and through the skill of psycho-therapy.

Poor Erica. She was brought up to be a 'proper' person, yet she became someone who felt unable to express feelings of affection.

Having low self-esteem

Barbara's presenting problem

Barbara came for help because she felt very depressed. At the start of our sessions she said: 'I feel very depressed, and useless. I have even wondered how much harm I have done to my own children because of my feelings of anger which seem to swirl about somewhere deep inside me. I feel that there is no way out for me. My doctor has prescribed drugs for years yet I do not seem any the happier. I am on imipramine [an antidepressant drug] and a combined oral contraceptive pill. My husband says that my depression is because of what happened when I was a child. I was deprived. I think that is the right word. I often think, if only I had received a good education, I would not be like this. I would have confidence, like educated people do. Also, I wouldn't then feel that everyone was looking at me and saying things about me, because then I would feel confident. Do you think I should ask for a change of drugs or should I have a go at alternative medicine?'

First, let me deal with certain misconceptions, and also with what should be an obvious area of enquiry concerning Barbara's problems. But because I am using the term 'misconceptions', do not for a moment assume that I would throw these back at the client as being matters she can just forget about, or just fling out of the window. These are very real concerns that she has, and many of you may have experienced similar ones.

First I would aim to help Barbara see that simply having a 'good education' would not have removed or prevented her feelings of depression and uselessness. But what about this word 'depression'? A lot of people tell us that they are suffering with depression and that their doctor has put them on antidepressant drugs such as imipramine. Most of these people are not in fact *clinically* depressed, although they are certainly people who feel depressed, low in spirits, fed up, and worthless – or, as Barbara put it, 'useless'. They are unhappy people, but they are able to talk with a therapist. They are willing to try out certain techniques in order to see if these will help them, and they have been motivated to come for help, whereas the truly clinically depressed person can be almost impossible to get through to. Dorothy Rowe speaks of the difference in this way:

> We say, 'I feel really depressed', when we mean, 'I'm unhappy'. Until we have actually been depressed we do not realise that there is a great difference between being depressed and being unhappy. When we are unhappy, no matter what terrible things have happened to us we still feel in contact with the rest of the world. When other people offer comfort and love we can feel it warm and support us.
>
> When we are depressed we feel cut off from the rest of the world. When other people offer us comfort and love, that comfort and love does not get through the barrier, and we are neither warmed nor supported. (Rowe, 1991)

To suffer real depression is to feel trapped in a black pit, or smothered by a thick, heavy material, or buried in a dark tunnel. It is to have no interest in anything or anyone, and no feeling of hope.

Barbara certainly said she had the feeling that there was 'no way out' for her, but she did seek help and could think about changing her medicine. In the way we use the term in our everyday language, she was 'depressed'. She was a very unhappy, downhearted person who felt useless, and inferior, but she was not clinically depressed.

Just a word about her medication. We are living in an age when the demand for drugs that will change or cure any condition is only excelled by the frenetic determination of the pharmaceutical companies to beat each other on the race to the next generation of drugs. As with psychotherapy, and surgery, etc., the use of pharmaceutical drugs and the skills and knowledge associated with their medical applications is God-given, but as with most skills, and most substances (even the purest foods), humans are capable of misusing them. It is interesting that while Barbara was on imipramine, an antidepressant drug, she was also taking a combined oral contraceptive pill. One of the possible side effects of 'combined' oral contraceptives (i.e. those containing oestrogen and progestogens) can be depression!

Would it have been different had Barbara already been a Christian? She says nothing about her religious beliefs, but it's possible that things might have been different.

However, and this may surprise some readers, it would not necessarily follow that she would have lost her feelings of depression had she had a strong Christian faith. Nor, for that matter, might it have made any difference had she been highly educated, or held a post of high responsibility, or both. These feelings deep inside her of, as she put it, uselessness, anger and depression are as common in schoolteachers, solicitors, professors, and others who have had an extended education, as they are in people with no academic qualifications who have left school as soon as they could.

Such feelings are also fairly common among Christians, even among those who have been called to preach and to minister to others. There is a wonderful Christian woman called Anne Townsend, and in her book *Faith Without Pretending* she recalls her feelings when depression and fear met her at a time when she had been a committed Christian for many years:

> The sense of isolation gripping me at this time was different from any aloneness I had previously experienced – different from being alone in my wooden Thai house [when she was a missionary] perched on its stilts on the edge of rice fields, after my miscarriage, after I sent my children away to boarding school in Malaysia or after friends had been killed in a road accident there. It seemed to me that no one else had ever passed

> through what I was going through. No one else could
> possibly understand my deep fear that the end result
> would be that I would be forever cut off from God. I felt
> as if I were the first person ever to be on the verge of
> stepping out from the haven (the 'sure salvation') of
> evangelicalism into . . . What? (Townsend, 1990)

But God has not left us without healing gifts for those who are
experiencing depressive feelings or clinical depressions, as
Anne Townsend seems to have been. Later in this book I shall
discuss these various paths to healing. But remember that
although God still works today through those who have his
special gift of direct healing (see the biblical accounts in Acts),
he also uses our knowledge of medicine, both orthodox (i.e.
state-registered doctors and nurses in the Western world) and
the so-called complementary therapies. Anne Townsend was
helped by the psychotherapy she received. Strong, and living
in faith, she says at the end of her book: 'The whole of the rest
of life still lies ahead. And I want to live it to the full.'

This present volume is not a textbook on psychology or
psychiatry and therefore I am avoiding lists of different types
or categories of depression. Furthermore, I am not assuming
that depressive moods, or real clinical depression, result only
from biological factors. It is an interesting fact that these days
it is not simply 'religious people' who subscribe to the view
that we are almost certainly more than the sum of various
chemicals, electrical impulses, synapses and brain cells.

Of course, our feelings and our thinking can be affected by
various chemicals (e.g. drugs), stimulants, and by environmental and biological factors ranging from atmospheric pollution
to having high or low blood pressure. We are, as long as we
are alive, holistic in the sense of being integrated – body, mind
and soul. Therefore, while accepting biological and social factors
as contributing to many experiences of clinical depression and
depression of mood, I am including factors contributing to
depression that do not spring from physical or environmental
needs. There is a human need that is purely spiritual.

Some of the most celebrated practitioners and theorists of the mind (e.g. Carl Jung, Viktor Frankl, Assagioli) reach out to the essential spiritual and holistic nature of humanity. Of course, they tend sometimes to use psychology jargon, so that we find Jung writing about 'individuation' (see Chapter Five), etc. But writers such as Frankl admit that there are situations involving conflict about meaning, about right and wrong, about sin, where real help is more likely when the physician is able to bring spiritual assistance because, as I would put it, God is using him or her as a channel. To quote from one of Frankl's books: 'The task [i.e. dealing with moral, ethical and existential questions] becomes equally easy for the doctor who happens to unite within himself the qualities of physician and religious person and who discusses questions of belief or value with patients of his own faith' (Frankl, 1973).

It is doubtful whether merely a change of drugs would be the answer to Barbara's problems. It may help for a time if she is suffering from side effects, but she also has a very low estimate of her own worth. Humility must not be confused with feelings of worthlessness. In God's eyes each of us is priceless, except in terms of the price paid by his Son. Barbara had 'learnt' that she was 'useless', and that there was 'no way out' for her.

Expert counselling or psychotherapy, and in some cases psychiatry with medication, may well help people like Barbara to get in touch with (i.e. become aware of) self-destructive elements in their mental make-up, and then to replace these by constructive elements: new attitudes, a fresh outlook. Often the self-destructive elements are attached to traumatic events, and the depressed person may still be dealing with the results of such events without even realizing it.

I shall close our discussion of Barbara's presenting problems with a quotation from a book written by a Christian psychiatrist, Dr John White:

The problem is always to treat the whole person without anyone else's help. I believe I can examine patients well, use appropriate tests and come to reasonable conclusions as to the nature of the problem. But to treat the suffering person may demand skills beyond those I possess . . . I also collaborate with pastoral and other counsellors. Shortage of time and a heavy schedule often hinder me from spending as much time as I would like with my depressed patients, and I may work with a counsellor, my role being more medical, while the counsellor or pastor may see my patient more frequently and deal with spiritual or psychological issues. (White, 1982)

Eating distress

Margaret's presenting problems

'I am a professional woman working in the hospital service, yet I often feel that my personal problems, which I keep very secret, are more burdensome than those that most of the hospital patients carry.

'I am in my late twenties, unmarried and without a boyfriend. I still feel very much a failure in life, even though I have a good job. I think that I should take some further training, partly to overcome this feeling of failure. It is not only a feeling of failure, but also a feeling of going through life like a cork tossed on the sea – just having to go with the currents.

'For several months now I have been secretly bingeing, stuffing myself with whole shopping lists of food and chocolates, and then feeling utterly guilty and making myself throw up – then feeling even guiltier about that. I just can't stand the idea of food inside me.

'Do you think that my further training idea will help me to overcome my problems?'

Before going further, let us look closely at Margaret's statement in order to isolate some very pertinent things she is saying. Let's, so to speak, read between the lines.

Her 'problems', whatever they are, have become associated with food, with eating. This is fairly common, and regretfully is becoming more so. Margaret refers to her problems as 'burdensome'; in fact, she feels she carries a heavier burden than most of the hospital patients she works for. She feels that she is a 'failure'. She talks about her life being akin to a cork tossed on the sea. This sounds as if she is not only drifting, but in some way feels trapped. In fact, she seems to feel she has no control over her life. And then she has this notion of further training. What for? Mainly, it seems, to help her overcome her problems!

How would further training help Margaret to stop bingeing and making herself vomit? The answer is that she feels it will be one more thing that will help her to *forget* her problems. She has already emphasized the fact that her personal problems are kept very secret. Margaret may have intended this to refer to her bingeing and making herself be sick (bulimia), but I would say that she probably has psychological problems that relate to factors that she needs to keep secret from herself. She is afraid!

Some people's problems are helped by them being guided to certain biblical passages that relate to some of the key words I have already highlighted. Words that relate to attitudes and feelings, such as: 'isolation', 'burdensome', 'failure', 'trapped' and 'fear'.

> So do not fear, for I am with you;
>   do not be dismayed, for I am your God.
> I will strengthen you and help you;
> I will uphold you with my righteous
> right hand. (Isaiah 41.10)

And words relating to burdens and feeling trapped:

> Take my yoke upon you and learn from me, for I am gentle and humble in heart, and you will find rest for your souls. For my yoke is easy and my burden is light. (Matthew 11.29–30)

Of isolation:

> For I am convinced that neither death nor life, neither
> angels nor demons, neither the present nor the future,
> nor any powers, neither height nor depth, nor anything
> else in all creation, will be able to separate us from the
> love of God that is in Christ Jesus our Lord. (Romans
> 8.38–9)

Such verses as these can be very uplifting and refreshing to
many of us when we may feel a bit depressed or disappointed.
And I recommend to Christians, and to those who are search-
ing for inner peace, such verses as these as well as many from
the psalms, especially if the searcher can come across them in
some guided study of Scripture rather than just as isolated
texts. (You will note that I have taken these comforting texts
out of context here and drawn on them in isolation. In
Chapter Five I shall give some consideration as to how and
why, in psychological terms, such texts can be beneficial.)

However, I want to go further with this discussion because
there are some psychological states, which any of us might
experience, whereby even if we accept these stupendous
truths, our emotional pain does not leave us. And this is not
because of a weakness in faith; rather, it is because of factors
that we are only beginning to understand. We are not talking
here about people who have neglected their spiritual welfare
(many in that category would certainly find their problems
dissolving if they were to turn to God), but those who
undoubtedly have faith, and yet who still feel as Helena
Wilkinson did about food. During her teenage years, Helena
almost died on account of her anorexia nervosa. Despite
having loving parents, she suffered traumatic experiences in
her early childhood. In her early adolescence she had a fear of
growing up and developed what she called a 'desperate search
for identity'. In her late teens she was hospitalized when she
had lost so much weight that her life was in danger. In her
book *Puppet on a String*, which she wrote when she was just
19, Helena puts her recovery down to her discovery of God's

love for her. Writing of the way she felt about food when she was at her lowest ebb, she says: 'I felt like a pig being fattened for eating. [She weighed about 6 stone instead of about 8½, the average for her height.] It was a horrible feeling, but when I tried to escape it I felt trapped. I was stuck in a maze, lost and confused, my life surrounded by paths leading to dead ends' (Wilkinson, 1984).

Before going further, it will be as well to define what is meant by the terms 'anorexia nervosa' and 'bulimia nervosa', usually referred to simply as anorexia and bulimia. In fact the two conditions are closely connected and very often exist together in the one person as a syndrome. They are examples of eating or feeding problems that in some way are associated with social or psychological factors.

In the case of anorexia, the person, usually a young woman – although not infrequently a young man – begins for some reason to limit the food intake. It may begin with some kind of dieting, but before long, if it continues, she starts to limit the food intake excessively. Then she will gradually develop guilt feelings about putting on any of the lost weight. As the illness develops, for by now we are talking of an illness, she begins to see her body as horribly, repulsively shaped, due, so she believes, to fat. Even when the sufferer – perhaps a young person of 5' 7" to 5' 10" in height – weighs only 5½ or 6 stone, she looks into the mirror and, despite the fact that her ribs are protruding, her legs look like bent bamboo rods and her eyes look sunken, she sees a revolting fat-laden image. Anorexics become secretive about their non-eating. They devise all sorts of stratagems to mislead parents and other concerned people. Moreover, they take to excessive exercise. They may, if they can't hide their eating or avoid eating, become bulimic – in that they make themselves vomit even the small intake of food that they are allowing themselves.

Bulimia may start with anorexia, as outlined above, but it can also develop as the first stratagem in a serious food intake problem. The bulimic, like the anorexic, develops an attitude concerning the body shape and size, but does not develop an

actual inhibition to food intake. Instead, she will first go
without food for several hours, maybe all day, during which
she thinks about the feast she is going to have later on. This
feast can be enormous, and usually includes many sweet and
sugary items. The bulimic will see herself eating cakes, bis-
cuits, chocolate, lots of bread, a pizza, cheese, sausages, crisps,
more cake, and so on. She will consume all this in one sitting,
and then have two or three pints of water. Then she will go to
the bathroom, put her finger down her throat, and be sick.
This goes on, in a seriously advanced case, day after day, week
after week. The bulimic becomes just as secretive as the
anorexic.

And, like the anorexic, the bulimic is in some way trapped
by the condition. She has developed a belief system concerning
her body, and how she relates to and is accepted by people in
her life. My patient, Margaret, when talking about her (presenting) problem, said, 'I just can't stand the idea of food
inside me.'

Margaret also asked a question. She said, 'Do you think
that my further training idea will help me to overcome my
problems?' But what were her problems? Yes, she was a
bulimic, but further study would not help with this, especially
as it had no relevance to bulimia. We should also bear in mind
that anorexics often have terrible mental conflicts connected
with food, and in later stages with ideas about recovering or
not recovering. They may desperately want to be normal in
their eating but they cannot be. That sounds a drastic thing to
say, but – as we shall find out as our study unfolds – people are
often trapped in a sort of double-wish syndrome that is not of
their conscious making – although it may well have developed
from quite an early period of their life.

Most people reading this will have experienced a certain
amount of compulsive thinking. You know the sort of thing
– when you feel you have forgotten to turn off the oven, but
you know really that you have. Some may even have experienced feelings that they might deliberately harm someone they
love; they know the thought is ridiculous, but it will not go

away. I shall discuss obsessional compulsive thinking later on. However, it is mentioned here to highlight the fact that very many people who are functioning well in society still experience feelings or 'beliefs' that seem to come along despite the fact that they do not want them to, and regardless of the fact that they don't actually hold these 'beliefs'! Now, if you can imagine turning up the volume of such feelings and beliefs ten- or twenty-fold, you will have some idea of what a real anorexic experiences, but you will still only have a vague idea unless you have actually been there.

There is a good deal of evidence to show that many cases of eating distress are associated with psychological, and especially emotional, development. This includes overeating as well as undereating. (There are other purely physical factors affecting appetite and malnutrition, but we are only concerned in this book with social and emotional problems and how they affect the lives of individuals and family groups.)

We have already quoted from Margo Maine's book called *Father Hunger*. This book focuses specifically on looking at the connection between distress in young women and girls and the relationship between them and their fathers. Here are a few more extracts from her text, and also from some of the girls and women concerned:

> Women who struggle with eating and body image problems often speak of unrequited love when they speak of their fathers. 'I never felt good enough for him' is a common refrain.

> *Quotation from sufferer*: When I was six years old my father told me I was too old to play with dolls. I never did again. I couldn't play. To gain acceptance from him, I had to act mature instead. I tried hard to win his approval. It may be why I became a lawyer. The only way to get his attention was to do something drastic. My weight loss was the only thing that ever worked in getting his concern. But then he was as angry as he was worried.

Quotation from another sufferer: I really wanted, needed, my dad to be proud of me. I wasn't sure how to get that – nothing I did seemed to work, but I knew he thought being thin was good, so I started to diet. It was the beginning of an eating disorder – but all I wanted was to please my dad. This was my only way to achieve. It showed self-control and all the things I thought he valued.

(Maine, 1993)

Just think back to what was briefly stated in Chapter One about the importance of attachment and the feeling of belonging and self-esteem, and note the importance of this final quotation from *Father Hunger* concerning self-control. The sufferer said, 'It showed self-control and all the things I thought he valued'.

There are, as I have said, many physical causes of food intake problems, and this includes wasting problems when people lose weight even when they are eating well. Because of this, it is important that people with eating or wasting problems should see their doctor. But let us look now at some of the attitudes and feelings so frequently reported by people with tendencies towards anorexia and bulimia, or the fully blown disorders.

Sometimes, for example, the sufferer feels a strange 'need' to keep the anorexic or bulimic state (or the overeating) because the misery resulting from it takes their mind off a bigger misery! This happens when people feel themselves under pressure or judgement from those who are important in their lives, such as parents or spouse, or when they feel themselves travelling down a path selected by other people. I once met a student at a highly reputed university. She hated the course, she hated the life, but instead of refusing to continue and establishing her own chosen path, she carried on – and at the same time 'forgot' the problems of university in the 'pain' of anorexia. It may seem a very strange way of behaving, yet in my work with disturbed infants, some of whom were neglected or abused, I have found something similar. I have met many infants who seemed to find it helpful, when under great stress, to damage themselves by pulling their hair out or deliberately crashing their heads against a solid wall. Clearly, much could be written on this subject, and much could be hypothesized, but in the case of infants harming themselves and adolescents starving themselves, there often appears to be a connection with an underlying psychological (emotional) problem. Helena Wilkinson was probably feeling this 'protection' afforded by the condition when she wrote: 'I wanted to get better, yet at the same time I was afraid of getting better; why, I don't know. I was in a dark tunnel and I did not know which end had the most light; which way should I turn?' (Wilkinson, 1984).

Another sufferer put it very strongly when she said, 'It [i.e. anorexia, etc.] anaesthetizes you from the pain you feel.' What 'pain'? Something you want to avoid?

Causative factors in eating distress

It would probably be quite wrong to ascribe any one factor as the 'cause' of eating problems. Setting aside (but not forgetting) that such problems do of course occur even in infancy, we must be concerned when we find that anorexia is developing even in girls as young as 11. Like certain other illnesses that appear to have a connection with the social life and family interaction of the sufferer, there are probably many causative factors, and something that is an important factor for one person may not figure at all in the eating distress of another. Take slimming, for example. Many anorexics give this as a starting point for their condition, yet almost as many say it never played a part at all. Often, slimming *does* come into it – there is some connection between losing weight and what a particular person has said about one's body shape. So we find girls and young women, and some young men, connect the start of their anorexia to an incident when they were called 'fatty' by a boy- or girlfriend, or a teacher. I know of one bulimic who traces the start of her illness to the time when her mother put her on a diet.

Yet how many people go on slimming diets without becoming anorexic? Certainly the social and peer group pressure these days to be thin (even to the extent of looking less attractive) is enormous and dangerous, but in most cases other pressures, psychological and social, are present – even though they may be unrecognized by the person themselves. Some anorexics, and even some of those who are medically trained, believe that anorexia may be traced to specific foods to which the person is allergic, or to foods that are addictive to individuals. However, there have been many disappointments in treating people entirely along these lines.

The same can be said of childhood insecurity, rejection, and loss through bereavement or separation as a result of divorce or desertion. These factors seem to play a major part in some cases. But other people, with similar backgrounds, have no eating distress. Fear comes into the list of causative factors too. Often the fear is a fear that they will fail either to satisfy the wishes and hopes of other people or their own strong internal demands. And while we are thinking about fear, it is reasonable to criticize some well-meaning Christian parents and teachers/ministers who have in effect brain-washed children into seeing God as an ogre waiting to devour them. They may have confused the idea of awe with fear so far as their teaching about God is concerned.

This fear of failure and the setting for themselves of high perfectionist standards sometimes relates to the subtle emotional blackmail used by parents to control children growing up. The issue of control appears to be important in anorexia, bulimia and other eating distress conditions. The anorexic may even be using her condition to control parents. Not that she necessarily does so to harm them. It may be, as we have seen, the only way of gaining attention. Let me hasten to add that most parents are not to blame for these conditions. The child often involves them, uses them, but, despite this, parents usually show enormous patience.

Many adolescents have a fear of growing up. This may relate more to the new and expected demands that they see ahead and feel they will fail to meet. Unconsciously, or at least subconsciously, the only control left is that of body control: stop it growing up, stop it developing!

Another factor that starts many people along the path leading to eating distress such as bulimia is that of comfort food. In a way this can be seen as a regressive act, a going back to the 'infant comforter' – and so many of us do it! When things have been stressful we might turn to a lovely chocolate bar or other sweets, or a 'naughty-but-nice' cake oozing with cream and jam. Very often the foods we choose are the addictive ones. Notice that I have more often than not used the expression 'eating distress' rather than 'eating problem', or 'sufferer'. 'Eating distress' is a term recommended by Carole Waskett who wrote a very helpful guidebook on the subject (Waskett, 1993).

The progression of eating distress

Fortunately most eating problems encountered do not greatly harm the individual who may be helped out of them or be strong enough not to let them take over their lives. But this should not lull us into overlooking the pain and danger associated with them. Anorexia and bulimia are serious conditions. All our problems may be taken to God, of course. If you have a health problem, you should usually – particularly if the illness is progressive and chronic – take yourself to the doctor as well as praying about it. But in most cases of eating distress that are severe and have turned into life-controlling issues, there will also be a need for skilled counselling or psychotherapy – and this does not mean that you are 'mental' or 'psycho'! Share your feeding distress with someone who has the time to work with you and has studied the condition, but first see your doctor. If you feel you can only share your problem with a therapist who is also a Christian, contact one of the organizations listed in Appendix A – but do make sure the person you go to is trained and qualified. (See also what I say in Appendix B concerning Christian counsellors.)

Gradually, the regular practice of doing a particular thing can turn into a habit (of behaviour or thinking), and a habit can turn into a form of control of self or others, and can later develop into a form of slavery. The word 'achievement' is pressed upon us more and more these days and is always associated with something good. However, it can take over a part of our lives in a most negative manner. So strong is this desire to achieve that a person who achieves a 'slimming' target of 8 stone can then develop an urge to slim down to $7\frac{1}{2}$ stone, then a drive to slim down to 7 stone – and so on to something under 6 stone. The drive by then is so great that any weight gained produces feelings of self-revulsion and guilt. Guilt feelings are definitely part of the experience of many anorexics and bulimics. By this stage, the person can also become depressed and 'jumpy'.

As the condition progresses and entraps the person, unrealistic ideas and feelings take over so that some people can reach a stage where a part of their 'self' begins to feel it might be better to die than to go on living. Along with the depressed feelings, a strange separation from the physical world can be experienced. Helena Wilkinson said, 'The whole world disappeared from me: I watched it shrink into the background becoming smaller and smaller' (Wilkinson, 1984).

When a young woman practically starves her body to death it is not surprising that gradually actual physical ailments can develop. One of the ways in which we know that a patient is recovering (as far as females are concerned) is that she starts to menstruate again after months or even years – for menstruation often stops in anorexic patients. But treating the body in this way can lead to many other conditions including throat bleeding, acne, shrinking ovaries, sterility, brittle bones, stomach rupture, epileptic fits, bloodshot eyes and, a typical symptom in advanced cases, the growth of lanugo hair, a sort of downy hair (as on a human foetus) growing at the back of the shoulders and neck, and on the upper legs.

I have spelt out these possible developments not to frighten readers, but to make sure that people are aware of the dangers of taking eating distress lightly. You yourself may not be affected, but you may be in charge of adolescents. Do pray about any youngster with even the beginnings of eating distress, and try to get her or him to share the problem, as I have outlined above.

Demon possession

It is at this point that something should be said concerning what is called demon possession, because I am aware that many Christians reading this book will have been told, often by people who are not really giving God's message, but their own, that the problems and illnesses we are describing are all due to spirit or demon possession, and that they should be exorcized. Now, just as we must be very careful and balanced concerning our diagnosis of psychological conditions and their treatment, so we must be very careful always to make decisions and judgements about demon possession only after much prayer and referring the problem to people known to have a special God-given gift in this direction.

We must also bear in mind, as we must with drug therapy, surgery, etc., that in the hands of incompetents or charlatans, enormous harm, if not evil, may result from inappropriately stating that a problem is the result of demon possession. Dr John White, a psychiatrist who is a Christian, has written: 'I have no question that demons are alive and well in the West.' He goes on, however, to warn: 'But some enthusiasts are exposed to danger, the danger of being mocked as fools by the very enemy they talk so much about, as well as of doing more harm than good. They seek to cast out demons where sometimes no demons exist. They may unwittingly pander to the weak conscious of some who want an excuse (an obliging demon) for what amounts to personal sin that needs to be confessed and put aside' (White, 1982).

Another Christian psychiatrist, Dr Gaius Davies, has recorded some information concerning a London clinic, which refers suspected demon-possession cases to a Christian minister working in a church centre. This minister is very skilled in exorcism and has a central place for prayer in his work. He reports that over 90 per cent of the cases he is asked to see suffer from a purely medical condition and do not need spiritual healing or exorcism (Davies, 1988, p. 209).

Margaret's presenting problems (which we looked at on p. 32) have given us a good deal to think about. Here was a professional woman with a very secret form of distress. She was, as she stated, 'secretly bingeing', stuffing herself with whole shopping lists of food and chocolates, after which she was making herself vomit. And then there were the feelings of guilt, a guilt one cannot separate from. If the bulimic eats and does not vomit, she feels guilty at having added food to her body; if she does make herself sick, she feels guilty about that too.

I am not presenting whole case histories in this book, but readers will appreciate by now that there can be many psychological and social factors involved in any eating distress, and clearly Margaret had reached a stage when she needed to discuss her feelings more deeply. This does not, of course, mean that the spiritual dimension is unimportant in eating distress cases.

In fact, one of the things that happens in eating distress is that the person begins to associate moral 'goodness' or 'badness' with food. 'I'm bad, or wicked, if I gain weight. I'm good if I lose weight.' Anorexics also develop the feeling that they have no right to need anything, and no right to feel happy. Many of these feelings may generate during adolescence or in earlier childhood when the developing child also carries inhibitions about discussing quite deep fears. Many readers will be able to say that they had anxieties and fears they never told anyone about, not even their parents or siblings.

Psychotherapy itself, depending upon the client's individual needs, may be incomplete without the therapist and the client reaching what we call an existential dimension, which may include the spiritual as well as the emotional aspects of life. The existential dimension will include thoughts about what we often call 'the meaning of life': 'What are we here for?' 'What is the purpose of life?' It also includes the way people 'see' and experience themselves and the world around them. Anorexics can develop a 'reality loss', so that no amount of looking into a mirror or at a photograph of their emaciated body will change their view of a fat and bloated image. They actually see this image, and feel it.

People in eating distress also develop skills at projecting images of themselves so as to put off people who might become alarmed. They may behave in such a manner that people, especially those outside the family, become impressed by what look like the behaviour patterns of a rather mature person. They may decline to be involved in the fun and games of adolescence and instead will be devoting their time to study or to expressing themselves in poetry or art. Often this becomes part of a genuine search for 'the real me'. They may not be sure whether they want to be controlling other people or to be controlled by others.

This identity search – 'Who am I?' or even 'Who do I belong to?' – can be part of an existential dimension, an existential need, which may be finally satisfied only in spiritual terms.

Where eating distress is present, therefore, we should do what we can to help the person concerned to obtain counselling from experienced and knowledgeable therapists as well as medical oversight by their GP. We should not deny them counselling, which may be used by God to help them. More than one sufferer has been helped by the therapist referring them to these comforting words of Isaiah:

But the Lord says,
'Do not cling to events of the past
Or dwell on what happened long ago.
Watch for the new thing I am going to do.
It is happening already – you can see it now!
I will make a road through the wilderness
and give you streams of water there.' (Isaiah 43.18–19, GNB)

Fears, phobias and panic attacks

Anne's presenting problems

'I am now 38 years old and have been mostly house-bound for the last two years. There is nothing wrong with me physically, and I have a faithful husband who does all the shopping, etc.

'I suppose my trouble is what people call agoraphobia, but I've only come to accept this in the last few weeks. All I can say is that when I'm indoors I feel safe. I don't feel happy, just safe from what's outside. As soon as I reach our gate I start to panic. I come out in a sweat and my heart starts to beat really fast. If I try to walk even a few yards, my legs turn to jelly. I'm even frightened that I might be going mad.

'Being a committed Christian I have prayed about my condition, and also various people have visited me from the chapel my husband attends – I can't cope with going there nowadays. They even brought a healer to me who practised the laying-on-of-hands, someone who I know for certain has helped others through this gift, but I am still the same.

'Is this all due to my own wickedness? Is it due to sin? Perhaps I have been unconsciously wicked – I know I have felt angry with God, and that is not allowed, is it?'

Notice, first, that Anne now believes that her trouble, as she calls it, is something called 'agoraphobia'. She says that she's at last accepted this diagnosis, if that is what it can be called. Before accepting this diagnosis, Anne had been convinced that she had a physical illness, if only it could be traced, and that she often thought she was likely to 'go mad', as she put it.

No physical disease was ever traced, at least not with certainty. There were several suggestions made by a number of different specialists, and she did have medication – some of it, with hindsight, being rather drastic. The side effects of the medication sometimes caused Anne to think that she'd been right all along to believe she had a physical disease, for her symptoms were now occurring all at once.

Notice also that Anne would get into a state that she called 'panic'. She was quite right to use that term, but she was wrong to think that because she had such fears (we call them *phobias*) and panic attacks, she was going mad. Panic states are very common, as are phobic states. It may not help someone a great deal just to know that other people have similar experiences, but it is important that sufferers get things in proportion and do not feel that phobic and 'jelly-legs' feelings are signs of madness. Clearly, it depends upon the intensity or the degree of these experiences as to whether professional help is required. Many people suffer some degree of fear and apprehension throughout their lives but they still manage to function OK. However, even when very intensive states of anxiety are experienced, as in Anne's case, there is a very high rate of positive response to treatment.

These sort of conditions do worry some believers a lot because they seem to be experiences that are the very opposite to what might be expected from having 'a faith'. How come I have so many fears and phobias, they say, when I have read Jesus' words: 'Do not be afraid, little flock, for your Father has been pleased to give you the kingdom' (Luke 12.32)? And why am I panicking when Jesus has said: 'Peace I leave with you; my peace I give you . . . Do not let your hearts be troubled and do not be afraid' (John 14.27)? In later chapters I shall look again at the theology of these verses, but at this point I simply want to help readers understand more about these human conditions. At the moment, though, it is enough to say that if you feel entrapped by these fears and panics, and want to lose them, you can be assured that God both understands and reaches out to you. He does not condemn you.

Anne said she felt she was experiencing something called agoraphobia. This is probably the most common phobia reported. But let us look first at what is meant, what is experienced, when the term 'phobia' is used, and then we can examine the 'panic function'. These two conditions often occur together, and in fact become so intertwined that they generate each other.

I am not talking here of the scary feeling that a lot of us get when we have to make a speech or when we are waiting at the dentist's. Sure enough, these are apprehensions and fears, but in a way they are more rational, more understandable than true psychological states of phobia, which often feel irrational and seemingly (until treated) uncontrollable. Here are a few wonderfully named phobias: claustrophobia – a fear of confined spaces; arachnophobia – a fear of spiders and creepy-crawlies; musophobia – a fear of mice; acrophobia – a fear of heights; scopophobia – a fear of being stared at; ereuthophobia – a fear of blushing; and erotophobia – a fear of physical love. There are many more, though.

For some people, the conditions I am talking about are not simply inconveniences, not simply a mild embarrassment at, for example, blushing. I am talking of conditions that may be so powerful, so crippling, that the patient can no longer continue at work; or, as in cases of erotophobia, are finding that their marriages are falling apart.

So far I have mentioned fears concerning actual objects, environmental conditions, and what might be called normal functions. I named fear of mice, and fear of physical love, for example. But there are other fears that people experience that seem, even to the person who experiences them, quite beyond the pale, completely unlikely, and yet so uncontrollable that they find it exhausting to carry on living. These are the compulsive obsessional thoughts, usually thought of as 'bad', 'wicked' or 'nasty', that arise again and again even though the sufferer feels they are 'silly'. Yet even these obsessional thoughts, in milder or less powerful forms, may sometimes be experienced by people who are not psychologically ill. A mother may experience a compulsive thought in which she feels she may injure or even kill her child. This may happen even when the child is greatly loved, and the mother knows that the thought is 'ridiculous', yet back it comes again. These obsessional thought fears (ruminative phobias) often concern doing harm to people one actually loves and has great affection for. I shall describe compulsive obsessional thoughts in greater detail in Chapter Three when discussing the presenting problems of Marilyn. For the present, though, I shall concentrate on fears concerning objects, situations, etc., as described above.

Anne said that she prayed about her agoraphobia, and so we must accept that, as a committed Christian, her prayers have been heard. She also makes it clear that she really wanted to rid herself of this condition.

Where might Anne's irrational fears have sprung from? First, let's look carefully again at what she says concerning her experiences. She said, 'As soon as I reach our gate I start to panic.' Here is a clue. Was Anne afraid of being outside, in town rubbing shoulders with the crowd, or was she frightened of re-experiencing the physical symptoms and terrible feelings she experienced last time she tried to go out? Was she afraid of feeling afraid? 'I come out in a sweat and my heart starts to beat really fast . . . my legs turn to jelly.' And, like so many people, when she had these feelings, Anne became afraid that she was 'going mad'. In fact, she was not going mad, and under totally different circumstances all these symptoms would have been part of a God-designed safety system. This I explain below.

Panic, the sort that Anne experienced, is connected with the learning process, briefly described in Chapter One. It is also connected with the automatic 'flight or fight' response I described in that chapter. Often, in cases like Anne's, a quite small matter triggers off feelings associated with actual memories of incidents that were frightening, or triggers off feelings associated with 'forgotten' incidents, incidents that have (for protective reasons) been pushed into the unconscious part of our mind or brain. The present incident may be something quite ordinary: the sight of snow, or a birthday, or perhaps a dead animal in the road. Such events can trigger off memories and dormant fears. When this happens, the 'flight or fight' safety mechanism rushes into action, with all its physical symptoms.

Then, because we are human and have the God-given gift of setting up belief systems (or becoming conditioned), we believe this will happen again as soon as we are outside the house. That belief now becomes a fear in its own right. So we become afraid to go out, and if we do go out, we immediately get the panic responses.

Sometimes an agoraphobic state is developed concerning a specific place, and then transferred or expanded in the mind to include all similar places. Kovel has reported a case in which a mother became unable to go into any car park, and then gradually the fear spread to almost anywhere. This poor woman also had some obsessional compulsive thoughts: '[she] was plagued with an unconscious hostility towards her infant, and had this feeling stirred up in a parking lot, thence forward had to avoid the parking lot. But she could avoid neither her hostility nor this pattern of dealing with it; and so found herself within a shrinking perimeter of forbidden areas until she finally had to remain confined to her bedroom' (Kovel, 1986, p. 58).

Because the panic state itself so often becomes the thing to be feared, I shall describe this state in a little more detail here. People have described their panic states to me and the more usual symptoms include breathlessness, a 'tight' feeling around the chest, sweating, palpitations, trembling, 'jelly-legs', dizziness, 'pins and needles', numbness in arms or legs, feelings of dread or fear, and sometimes a feeling of 'unreality' about things.

Panic may be felt by anyone. The first experience may occur after a distressing event – although not necessarily immediately after; it could occur some months later – or it may appear to come 'out of the blue', or from a disturbing thought. The person can then become 'sensitized' which means that the smallest suggestion of the feared thing causes a learned response and then, partly because people think it is going to get worse and worse, a full panic state is reached.

It is possible for people to get on to the 'panic cycle'. For example, a young man came for therapy because he was feeling very anxious. He also thought he might be having a heart attack or that his lungs might stop working. His doctor had previously given him sedatives (tranquillizers). This young man described to me certain 'stressful' situations during which he was likely to go into full panic. He liked watching football matches, yet one of his panic situations was being at a match, and he was especially panic-prone at exciting moments in the game. It was at such times that he would become breathless, have palpitations, and feel that he was about to go mad or even to die. Sometimes he had to leave in the middle of the game. This meant he became 'programmed' to the idea that at football matches he'd go into a panic. One way in which I was able to help him – as well as through desensitization, which I describe below – was to assist him in developing a different attitude towards the initial changes occurring in his body during excitement. No doubt a lot of the other spectators felt their hearts race as the match got exciting, but they viewed this as normal. Our young man didn't. He went on to a full panic because he believed (and feared) these automatic body–mind responses were a form of physical illness.

Gradually he was able to accept, and expect, these accelerated body functions as normal, and to wait for them to die away. In this way he moved from the panic cycle and into the alternative (neutralized) cycle (see diagram on p. 52).

There are other ways in which people may be helped if they are experiencing irrational phobias. One method used by psychologists and psychotherapists is called *desensitization* and it involves a form of retraining or relearning. The therapist, with the sufferer's agreement, subjects the person to a small exposure of the feared object or situation, while at the same time, and this is important, helping her/him to keep relaxed with that small amount of exposure. Gradually most people are able to increase the exposure yet still keep calm. Eventually they

PANIC: Could this be what's happening?

A

An event that 'naturally' may carry some (healthy) stress or excitement occurred, or is expected to occur.

Note:
This is usable so long as the client's physical condition is OK and his/her doctor says there's nothing physiologically wrong.

━━━━━▶ = Panic cycle

┈┈┈┈▷ = Alternative (neutralized)

B

Such events produce body sensations associated with excitement, e.g. increased heart rate, breathing changes, sweating, trembling, etc. This is a *normal* process, stronger in some than others.

Neutralized cycle

Panic cycle

B+

Alternative to 'C'

'OK, I feel these body changes more than some people. These are *normal* changes and will *not* grow and grow. If I wait and relax my muscles, the sensations *will* pass.'

Panic cycle

Alternative thinking

C

But the person thinks: 'I should not have these sensations, something terrible is about to happen such as heart failure, a stroke, going mad!' etc. This is not true.

D

PANIC STATE

Because this person *felt* 'B', and *thought* 'C', his/her autonomic (glandular) mechanism (for 'fight' or 'flight') takes over.

Adrenaline is produced, the heart speeds up, breathing may change, legs may feel like jelly, etc. (all temporary). So now s/he is set to stay on the *panic cycle*.

The panic cycle

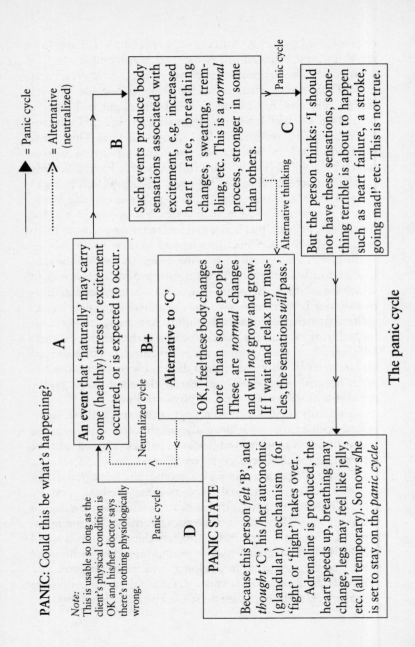

are able to tolerate full exposure and to remain calm and relaxed. The very experience of such calmness in the presence of the previously abhorrent object or situation produces another degree of confidence. If the sufferer believes in the power of prayer, then they can be greatly helped by prayer and meditation during exposure. This, of course, assumes that the therapist also believes in the validity of prayer.

Even though the sufferer may *feel* out of touch with God, prayer, alongside other treatments, is very helpful:

> Lord
> I can't go on
> Meaning has left everything and I don't know
> What I can do.

> Here, Lord,
> I will just drop
> Into the abyss
> Into the fullness of your hand.

> Here, Lord,
> I will stand empty
> I am waiting to be rescued
> But can't wait much longer.

> Here, Lord,
> I am drowning,
> But I will believe
> That it is in the fullness of your love.

(Schaffer, 1983)

This brings us on to Anne's worries about the possible connection between her agoraphobia, her 'own wickedness', and her anger towards God. She asks four questions, two direct and two implied. Is it due, she says to my own wickedness? Is it due to sin? Have I been unconsciously wicked? And am I allowed to be angry with God?

Let's consider the second of these questions first: is it due to sin? The biblical answer to this question is surely 'yes'. But we need to be clear that we are talking here about all that is *imperfect* in God's eyes both morally and physically. We are referring to 'inherited sin' or evil (imperfection), which according to the Bible entered into the whole global system as a result of Adam's rebellion. From that moment on there resulted a universal blight in which we all share, and which spoils that which God created 'perfect' (yet free to sin or not to sin). So the answer to that part of Anne's questioning is, yes, as a consequence of evil there is wicked behaviour, foolish behaviour, 'blind' or unwise behaviour, suffering, disease and, yes, agoraphobia! But this does not necessarily result directly from wickedness on the part of the sufferer. In a universal sense we are all slaves to sin. As with St Paul: 'We know that the law is spiritual; but I am unspiritual, sold as a slave to sin. I do not understand what I do. For what I want to do I do not do, but what I hate I do' (Romans 7.14–15).

But Anne's first question was: 'Is it due to my own wickedness?' This touches upon a more narrow theological question, which asks: 'Whenever we are ill or have strong fear or anxiety, is this the direct result of our individual sin? Is this some sort of direct punishment?' Let's look a little closer first at what we shall call *personal sin*. We can distinguish behaviour that makes it possible for us to categorize personal sin in the following manner:

1 Deliberate, conscious, wilful acts that are contrary to God's (biblical) teaching. We can call these 'sins of commission'.
2 Behaviour that is contrary to God's teaching (against God's nature), but that results from our failure to carry out God's commands or our failure to live according to his wishes and ordinances. In other words, we may sin in what we fail to do, rather than in what we do. These may be called 'sins of omission'.

However, person-to-person sin and group sin, where a whole society or culture is involved, both infects and affects 'innocent' people (i.e. innocent of a particular act or failure).

Moreover, such sin can have the effect of causing the 'inno-cent' person to have feelings of guilt. Person-to-person sin is often a combination of 1 and 2 above. I have met adults who, as children, had the most outrageous things done to them. As a result, they suffered all sorts of anxieties, phobias, depres-sion and other conditions. They would have been totally wrong in thinking that their condition was a punishment from God in a direct way. They certainly suffered as a result of sin – someone else's sin! And maybe the people who ill-treated or neglected them (a sin of omission) had also suffered in the same way. Therefore we are all enmeshed in sin. (I shall pick up this theme again in Chapter Five).

Other people may suffer, and be emotionally wounded, as a result of not having received what God intended they should receive. In Chapter One I outlined the importance of 'good-enough' child nurture and attachment experience. Sometimes parents unwittingly fail their children in this respect. They may have been emotionally injured themselves to the extent that they display no affection for their own children. Therefore such children suffer as a result of sin. Clearly, then, sin is not only a so-called 'wicked deed'. It also includes all that is contrary to the wishes of God, and goes against his design for human living and responsibility for the care of his world.

The guilty feeling that Anne was carrying – that is, the feelings resulting from the idea that 'Because I have sinned, God has sent agoraphobia to punish me' – was inappropriate guilt. We have all heard of people who felt guilty because they emerged alive from a car or train accident, whereas their friend, or the other passengers, died. Some of these people have seen the accident as being in some way their fault, even when it concerned a plane, ship or train. I am aware of a children's residential home where the cook died as a result of an illness. Some of the children felt guilty (a common feeling in a grief situation) and blamed their 'naughtiness' for the cook's death. 'God', they said, 'may punish us.' All quite untrue, and unfair to God, but this is how the mind may work.

Anne's agoraphobia was not a punishment sent from God – in his wisdom he could use even her agoraphobia.

Paul Tournier, a doctor and the author of several Christian books, has written:

> I was once told that a sister in a religious order brought a sick person one of my books and said to him: 'Here. Read this book, and you will realize that you must be a sinner, because you are ill'. That anyone should think me capable of writing such a thing! . . . It is true that we cannot over-emphasize the harm done by such theories, completely unsupported as they are by the Bible. (Tournier, 1983)

Anne had one more concern about her relationship with God. She said: 'I know I have felt angry with God, and that is not allowed, is it?' Poor Anne, what kind of a heavenly Father did she imagine she had? What kind of a God do people think Jesus represented? Is God, the Father of the Son of Man, such a petty peevish little God that he will smack you down if you feel angry? Are love and anger to be so separated? Which of us has not felt anger towards those we love?

Human anger, of course, is often associated with a lack of understanding, and with actual misunderstanding. But anger itself, as Gary Collins says, is 'an attribute of God and a common, probably universal, experience of human beings' (Collins, 1989). He goes on to say, 'Anger is a God-given emotion that, in itself, cannot and should not be eliminated or prevented.' It is not our anger that is bad, it is the destructive and hurtful way we often use it. Elsewhere in this book, however, I comment upon our need to learn to control our impulses, including anger impulses.

The Bible speaks of several of God's servants who at some time or other experienced angry feelings (misplaced of course) towards God. But God did not reject them on that account. The better known of these are Jonah, who became quite angry with God because he did not punish the 'wicked' people of Nineveh (Jonah 4.1–2), and Job, who ranted at God: 'Do not condemn me, but tell me what charges you have against me. Does it please you to oppress me, to spurn the work of your hands, while you smile on the schemes of the wicked?' (Job 10.2–3). Then there was Elijah. Perhaps his was indignation rather than anger: '"I have had enough, Lord," he said. "Take my life; I am no better than my ancestors"' (1 Kings 19.4).

You will recall that I spoke of certain defence mechanisms in Chapter One. There is one mechanism, or learnt way of behaviour, that is called *displacement*, and another is called *projection*. These behaviour functions are often seen in anger. When we are angry with certain people, events, or our own poor functioning, we tend to displace our anger on to someone else. We project it on to a third party. Consciously we are blaming someone else (not seeing the plank in our own eye!) and it is very easy at times to displace our anger on to God. Of course God would prefer that we had no need to displace our anger on to him, but he does not strike us down, nor reject us if we are confused enough to do this. And he would not reject Anne just because – like Job – she misplaced her anger.

Irrational fear, phobic experience and feelings of panic may be mild, or not very important, in some lives (fear of snakes will not greatly affect people, who can easily avoid them), but they may be devastating and crippling experiences for others. You may find that your particular experience is that these feelings are overcome or removed by reasoning or prayer, or by God's grace through his power of direct healing. You may perhaps find that a short course of drug therapy helps you, again God-guided. However, you may also find that these things do not remove your problem. As we have said, you need not associate this with particular acts of wickedness. Do not be shy to seek counselling or psycho-therapy, or be quick to believe that God excludes the use of such help.

Remember, these conditions may relate to experiences that are 'forgotten' or alien to God's purpose, but have, for protection, been partly repressed – but are still active enough to cause problems.

Relationship dynamics, and the influence of the pre-menstrual syndrome (PMS)

Ron's and Sally's presenting problems

Ron: 'Sally is my girlfriend. She is divorced and has one child, a lad aged nine. I wanted to marry Sally, but we have been rowing so much recently that I feel it might not work. We are living together, at least we were, but we split up last week – just to cool off I think.

'I don't understand Sally. She used to be really sweet, I mean sort of chirpy and full of fun. She was also very much what I saw as my little girl. Now I sometimes say, "Where's that angel of mine gone to?"

'I'm in business and have to work late quite often, so I have put off joining her in the evenings – sometimes until quite late. On the other hand, I try to keep weekends clear. But if things go slightly wrong, Sally doesn't just get cross, she goes mad. She'll throw things about – smash up furniture. She even rammed the car into a brick wall in a temper. And when she gets like that I can't speak to her.

'She's also suspicious of me. Doesn't trust me – at least, she doesn't when she gets into one of these moods. She's even arrived at the office and shown me up because she imagined I was having affairs with other women. The last time her language was so bad my boss called me in about it.

'Recently I've not been able to get on with her little boy, Peter. He's very spoilt by Sally's mother, and I think she tends to take the kid over. I get on with Sally's mother all right, but only because I avoid challenging her. As a matter of fact Sally's mother is good to her. She's always around helping out, and gives Sally all sorts of advice about housekeeping, gardening and all that. For some reason, Sally seems scared of her.'

Sally: 'Yes, I agree that I do get into uncontrollable bouts of temper, but the trouble is that there is something wrong with me. When that happens it's not really me – not my normal self. People don't seem to understand I'm ill. Ron doesn't appreciate that. Sometimes I feel trapped in life, like I must escape. That's one reason why I'm so careful with my mother. I don't want to upset her, she's been so kind, but she doesn't understand either. She comes and says the house is untidy or that Peter's clothes are not right, too small or a bit worn. Sometimes she says I'm not feeding him properly or he's up too late. I keep telling her I intend to do this or that when I get round to it, but that I've been ill – I'm often feeling tired and ill. And Peter is getting so disobedient. He threatens to tell his gran about me so I have to give in.

'I also feel that I've got to get people off my back. I want to do my own thing and be *me* for a change. I've started going to church. My mother is against this. Ron says he doesn't mind, but then he says, "Why do you do things now which cause rows? Where has my little girl gone who used to be so sweet?" I have to pacify everyone, Ron, Mother, Peter, the lot . . . I'm at breaking point.'

The statements made by Sally and Ron will have helped you to identify quite a number of the problems – or, at least, the surface problems. Ron seems to be missing for long periods of time. He puts it down to his business. But Sally actually agrees that she has these terrible tantrums, bad enough to make anyone keep clear.

Sally's mother looms large in this family, and lots of 'observers' – friends or relatives, for example – feel that she is doing a 'marvellous job' under difficult circumstances. It is also noticeable that Ron keeps talking about his 'little girl' – that is, the Sally that was – and that he has a difficult relationship with

Sally's son, Peter. This case brings out the complexity of what we shall call inter-person relationships. Such factors are usually present in any situation, but this case highlights the interactional factors.

We must not, however, overlook the fact that as well as psychological factors, there may also be environmental and actual physical factors that are causing tension and distress. In the presenting problems an important factor was not mentioned until later in the therapy. Sally, in fact, suffered enormously from a condition known as premenstrual syndrome (PMS), sometimes just referred to as PMT (premenstrual tension). I am not in any way being sexist here – in fact, I am taking up Sally's own point. Of course, there were other factors, which I shall discuss, but it would have been unfair to have discounted what she felt was a physical illness: a condition that affected her psychologically. So I shall deal with this condition – or, rather, the behaviour and feelings that can result from it – in general terms first. Before going further, though, I should emphasize that PMS is a condition that should first be treated by the sufferer's doctor.

Medical practitioners who do accept PMS as an illness (and not all do) see it as a hormonal disturbance. There are many symptoms associated with the condition, and a sufferer will most likely experience only some of the symptoms, which include certain psychological or 'emotional' states: irritability, aggression, moodiness, argumentativeness, tearfulness, loss of interest in sex, a craving for sweet things. There are, of course, many physical symptoms associated with PMS, including: headaches, asthma, rhinitis and dysmenorrhoea (painful periods).

As in the case of phobias and eating distress that we looked at earlier, it is a matter of degree as to whether or not premenstrual discomfort or tension becomes an 'illness' or a disease (dis-ease). Most women are not unduly affected. However, for a minority, the effects can be almost catastrophic, and the worst aspect is that the cause of their erratic behaviour can be overlooked. Nowadays PMS is defined as the recurrence of symptoms (listed above) before menstruation, with a complete absence of symptoms after menstruation. Dr R. Simpson states:

This definition means that:

1 The symptoms occur exclusively in the second part of the menstrual cycle (the luteal phase).
2 There is a common absence of symptoms after the onset of the heaviest day of menstruation for at least 7 days.
3 Symptoms recur during three successive menstrual cycles.

Using this definition all chronic illnesses are excluded because the complete absence of symptoms for at least seven days excludes chronic physical and chronic psychological illness. (Simpson, 1992)

I have spelt out these details of PMS because when the condition is serious, the effects really can be devastating – and this was so in Sally's case. Normally she was a reasonable person, managing her family and doing her part-time job in a cool, pleasant manner, but she would suddenly turn into a person who, in her jealousy and irrational thinking and rage, would smash up her furniture, accuse her loved ones of wicked deeds, and end up crying and feeling suicidal. And this was not caused by the devil or spirit possession, despite the similarity of behaviour in certain cases.

Dr Katharina Dalton, who specializes in this condition at the Premenstrual Syndrome Clinic, University College Hospital, London, writes: 'PMS can ruin relationships, affect other members of the family and play havoc with career prospects. Sufferers deserve effective progesterone treatment which is available within the NHS rather than rely on the unproven supplementation of vitamins or minerals as advocated by entrepreneurs and sponsored by the media' (Dalton, 1990).

Sally's PMS, however, was not the only factor involved in wrecking the family unity, although readers will by now recognize the importance of dealing with her extreme example of the condition that seemed to undo all the good that might have been coming from psychotherapy or family counselling.

So let's have a closer look at Ron's part in all this. On the face of it he seems (and probably feels) hard done by and very reasonable, but he has certain worrying attitudes. He harps on about Sally as his 'little girl' and asks 'where has she gone to?'

This made me wonder how much of a juvenile role Ron saw Sally playing. It could also, I felt, relate to the way Sally had always had to be the 'little girl', even when she was grown up but lived with her parents. But more on this in a moment. I was also interested in the way Ron related to Sally's mother. He said he got on all right with her because he avoided 'challenging' her. Does that sound like the peacemaker? Does that make you think of the verse 'Blessed are the peacemakers' (Matthew 5.9)? I wonder whether that is correct thinking in this context? We shall see.

So what about Sally's mother, who was, according to Ron, always around and 'helping out', and giving marvellous advice about gardening and housekeeping. Why on earth was Sally so scared of such a wonderful mother? Even Peter, who was getting 'so disobedient', used to call on his wonderful grandmother.

Of course I have been giving you the presenting problems, the events and behaviour that Sally and Ron explained when they first came for treatment. And already we have seen that a most important factor, PMS, was missing from that list of the things that were 'wrong'. Now we can look at a few more 'missing facts'.

First, what did Sally's childhood reveal? She was an only child, and her mother seems to have been fond of telling her that she disliked children once they were past the first 18 months of life, and that she only had Sally as a sort of insurance in case she lost her husband. She couldn't bear the idea of being on her own.

Both parents created an entirely artificial environment in the 'home', turning it into a mini Ideal Home Exhibition –

where nothing could ever be a centimetre out of place. In fact, as an example of the extreme fastidiousness, Sally told me that there were decorative rugs dotted around, which as a child (and as an adult) she was forbidden to step on! This caused great inconvenience when she was unable to stretch across to turn on a switch or reach for something beyond the rug.

Sally's father, she said, was a weak character, completely dominated by his wife (Sally's marvellous mother). He went along with all she said until one day he gave himself to Christ, as Sally put it, at a Billy Graham rally, and joined a church without the consent of his wife. Sally's mother was furious both with God (whom she did not believe was there!) and with her 'stupid' husband. From then on she tried to make his life miserable. But, said Sally, it didn't seem to work; he seemed to have 'found something'. A year later, when Sally was 14, her father died of cancer.

Sally's mother then concentrated all her 'love' on her daughter. She told her which classmates she could have as friends and which ones she must cold-shoulder, what clothes she was to wear, what 'healthy' food she was to eat, what food was to be avoided, and so on.

Sally had always been afraid of her mother. She was riddled with irrational guilt feelings if ever she attempted to do anything without first obtaining her mother's approval. Her mother also exercised an exquisitely cruel form of emotional blackmail. She would say to Sally, 'What would your father have said if he had seen you out with ——?' and she'd name some perfectly likeable and reasonable acquaintance.

This gives you a brief insight into Sally's childhood. However, the feelings of subordination and fear concerning her mother were carried over into adulthood. When she and Ron came to me, this was the emotional relationship between mother and daughter.

The control practised by Sally's mother over her daughter extended not only into Sally's adulthood but into the deep recesses of her mind. She was, in fact, despite having been married, a mother, an adult, terrified of her mother's disapproval. And her mother, not even recognizing her own sinful behaviour – for that is what it amounted to – continued to make demands upon Sally concerning the way she, Sally, ran her home and brought up her son. Sally was very uneasy during one of her therapy sessions because she had not cut the grass, as instructed by Mum two days previously, and Mum was visiting that very day!

No wonder Sally said, 'Sometimes I feel trapped in life, like I must escape.' But was she right to go on to say, 'That's one reason why I'm so careful with my mother'? What did she mean by being 'careful'? Whatever she thought she meant at that time, it became clear as the therapy developed that 'being careful' amounted to giving up her own self-identity and remaining to all intents and purposes a child – and a child without many rights and with little self-determination. To Sally, this careful (daughterly?) treatment of her mother looked like love. To disregard one's parent – to tell her mother, however kindly, to stop interfering – looked like some form of ingratitude and sin.

There are many cowed Christians who think in this same way. Here are some words to ponder, gleaned from a small book by Denis Duncan: 'It is wise to remember C. Day Lewis' words, "Selfhood begins with a walking away and love is proved in the letting go". Love as kindness is never a smothering process. It is a cultivating one. It never aims to bind, only to liberate. It is not offered as an order to be obeyed, but as a gift to be received' (Duncan, 1981).

Sally saw only what she called her mother's 'kindness'. In fact, that was the way she had been taught to see all her mother's behaviour. I spoke of the learning process in Chapter One. Sally actually experienced frustration and anger, and because of such feelings she also felt guilty.

Ron also failed to recognize the insinuative and manipulative power of Sally's mother. 'For some reason,' he said, 'Sally seems scared of her.' He also saw what he interpreted as Peter, Sally's son, being 'spoilt' by his grandmother. But here in fact was another take-over. Not only was Sally's mother using her parent power to deprive her daughter of her sense of *being*, but she was ready to capture her grandchild and to use him as a further form of control.

So, without extending unduly the discussion of this case and the principles at work in the inter-person relationships, how could Sally and Ron be helped in so far as therapy was concerned? I cannot deal here with the actual therapeutic stages or techniques, but it will be clear to most readers that the people involved in this situation all needed to change. Their ideas needed to change, their attitudes needed to change, and above all their behaviour needed to change. As in many of these situations, the main sufferer needed to change drastically. God did not intend that Sally should go through life unable to function as a reasonable and, to some degree, a self-determining person. But when sufferers like Sally are helped to change, those around them, for insidious reasons often unrecognized by themselves, may violently oppose the change. They may even accuse the therapy or the therapist of having made matters worse. Imagine Sally's mother in a situation where Sally suddenly found the strength to say, 'By all means come to my house, Mum, we love to see you, but from now on understand things here are going to be run the way Ron and I decide, and if I let the grass grow wild, that's how it will be.'

As a matter of fact, Sally had to be helped to ignore a tactic, a sin, often employed by her mother, who would, to put it bluntly, sulk! If ever Sally tried to be '*me* for a change', her mother would storm out and wait for her daughter to phone her up and apologize through her tears – the guilty one!

But in therapy Sally did change: 'I've started going to church. My mother is against this.' She was about to stop going, and once more to lose her identity, but this time she did not stop. A change had begun. Who are we to say just how God brought about this change. Did God use Billy Graham – and only Billy Graham? Or did God also use the skills he has allowed me as a psychotherapist? Did he use both? Only he knows.

Before closing the discussion based on this case, I feel it is important to look further at Ron's role in the unhappy state of affairs. Admittedly, he was not to blame for Sally's PMS, but he certainly went along with the idea that Sally should not change. He several times referred to her past personality as 'my little girl'. In a way, he did not want her to become emotionally grown up.

Ron's attitude to Sally's mother also needed to change. He had a life of his own, and this meant he mostly arrived home too late to have any real involvement in family life. So having plenty of scope for self-expression in business, he 'got on' with Sally's mother because, as he put it, he avoided challenging her. He opted for a peaceful existence, which he did not in fact get, and ironically he felt he was being wise in allowing Mum to crush Sally.

Avoiding challenging people who are destroying you, or someone you love or wish to help, is not the act of a peacemaker. This is not what Christ meant by 'Blessed are the peacemakers'. Whether she knew it or not, Sally's mother behaved towards her daughter in a sinful way. This should have been challenged. Much later, when Sally responded to treatment and became a Christian, this became possible.

From reading the discussion concerning this case history and the four others reported in this chapter, it should have become clear that as well as individuals being affected (you could say *infected*) by various very personal and idiosyncratic behavioural reactions, there is also the dimension of inter-person activity. From birth onwards there is an interactive process going on. The infant is *acted upon* by the adults and siblings who surround her/him, and at the same time the infant *reacts* to those around her/him. All the psychological processes outlined in Chapter One are active. Sally, for example, *learnt* a certain way of responding to her parents. Unfortunately they had learnt how to misuse the nurturing process. And, yes, the process of attachment was involved. Sally certainly showed a form of attachment to her mother, albeit that it was a faulty state of attachment. She could be said to have had attachment problems.

I shall continue, over the next two chapters, to examine and discuss the outcome of several other presenting problems. I shall do this in the light of Bible teaching and remembering that, 'The Christian life must be viewed as a vigorous journey and one that takes daily discipline, especially the discipline of self-control' (Shields and Bredfeldt, 2001, p. 505).

Three

Peace of mind makes the body healthy.

Proverbs 14.30 (GNB)

It would be quite wrong to think that human problems come in neat packets in the way they seem to come in the pen-pictures I am presenting. In Barbara's case, in Chapter Two, depression was the main problem I focused on, whereas with Margaret it was to do with her eating distress. But of course depression (or a miserable feeling of unhappiness) may also be present where an eating disorder such as bulimia or any other condition is prevalent. In the relationship problems of Ron and Sally, for example, some forms of depression were there too.

The different conditions described in Chapter Two and in this chapter are likely to appear in all sorts of combinations, even though it is often possible to focus on only one or two of these conditions in a particular case. Take *panic*, for example. My illustration in Chapter Two centred on Anne and her panic state, but a 'feeling of panic', and sometimes real panic states, may affect people whose lifestyles and situations are totally different from Anne's.

In this chapter I shall focus, in one case, on the strong inferiority feelings experienced by one person, and on the morbid thoughts another described as part of her problem. It is easy to see, though, that with some people both morbid thoughts and feelings of inferiority may go together. People often experience an assortment of the conditions I am describing. We may almost picture them as different ingredients, which make up the 'pudding' of feeling experiences, or we may think about them as different colours that mix together in a thousand ways to produce many pictures. Mark, the subject of my next pen-picture, suffered from conditions that are common in varying degrees across a spectrum that ranges from wealthy professionals to those living in total poverty: feelings of inferiority, inadequacy and shyness. In Mark's case his shyness was combined with a firm belief that he was a hopeless case – someone who couldn't be changed or helped.

Shyness and lack of confidence

It is easy to think of shyness as something either to be lightly dismissed or smiled upon in a vaguely patronizing way as people do with shy children. We even find clever humorous writing about the subject of shy people. Here's a brief extract from Charles Dickens's sketch on 'The Bashful Young Gentleman':

> The young gentleman seated himself at the table with evident misgivings, and turning sharply round to pay attention to some observations of his loquacious neighbour, overset his bread. There was nothing very bad in this, and if he had had the presence of mind to let it go, and say nothing about it, nobody but the man who had laid the cloth would have been a bit the wiser; the young gentleman in various semi-successful attempts to prevent its fall, played with it a little, as gentlemen in the streets may be seen to do with their hats on a windy day, and then giving the roll a smart tap in his anxiety to catch it, knocked it with great adroitness into a tureen of white soup at some distance, to the unspeakable terror and disturbance of a very amiable bold gentleman, who was dispensing the contents. We thought the bashful young gentleman would have gone off in an apoplectic fit, consequence upon the violent rush of blood to his face at the occurrence of this catastrophe. (Dickens, 1836)

But deep feelings of inadequacy, inferiority and shyness can become a torture to some people. These feelings may affect their work life and their social life, setting up actual physical stress in many cases. 'Why has God made me so shy?' said a

Christian friend to me a while ago. 'I crack up if I'm expected to pray out loud at a meeting, and I have lots of things I'd like to say at Bible study groups but I remain silent.' The fascinating thing is that even if we *remain* timid, God can use us. Recall the story of Moses and his worry about his speaking ability: 'But Moses said to the Lord, "Since I speak with faltering lips, why would Pharaoh listen to me?"' (Exodus 6.30).

Remember that all the way through history God has surprised humanity with *his* choice of whom he calls for a particular role. So let's look again at a few of the presenting problems, and some of the many variables involved.

Mark's presenting problems

'I have no confidence at all. I put this down to my basic personality, something I was born with, I suppose. I've always been shy, yet I take on tasks, and employment, that make me feel worse. I trained as a salesman, but I had to give the job up because I just lost confidence, just went to pieces.

'What with this and my hopeless sense of judgement, really I am hopeless, and I often make wrong choices. I know I'm hopeless. I know that when things go wrong, people decide to cancel dates with me, or worse, just not turn up. It must be me. It must be my fault. I'm a pretty hopeless person but, like I say, I seem to have been born that way! I'd really like to come across as slick, even tough, but I finish up like a pathetic infant! As a Christian this upsets me too, because the Bible actually tells us to be meek and mild, and as a result I finish up a nervous wreck. Should I take a course in assertiveness training?'

This must be one of the most negative statements so far reported in this book. Poor Mark is convinced that all the things that 'go wrong' in his life are his fault (i.e. he is blameworthy), and what's more it is all because of what he was 'born with'. He does express a glimmer of hope in that he thinks it is just possible that something called 'assertiveness training' may be able to bring about some changes.

This last idea is interesting because he has already put everything down to his basic personality, which he seems to think cannot be changed. This idea is worth considering – can his *personality* be changed? Some people do not like the idea of changing one's personality – it sounds dangerous. But if we put it a different way, it may become acceptable: if we say we would like to be able to change our *behaviour*, or for some other folk to change their behaviour, that seems more acceptable. Most of us believe that, at least to some extent, behaviour can be changed – so, for that matter, may beliefs and attitudes.

One thing I do not wish to do here is to start defining what is meant by the term 'personality'. Even the experts get into a twist if they try this one, and yet these days we use the word frequently; it is a household word – 'Hasn't she got a nice personality!' or 'He's got no personality, that's the trouble', and so on.

For many years now psychologists have been arguing over how much of our behaviour, feelings, reactions, anger, sympathy, humour, sadness, intelligence, and the rest of ourselves, is due to what we were born with (i.e. *nature*) and how much is due to what we have learnt from our life experiences (i.e. *nurture*). In fact, this was known as the nature–nurture argument, and if you are clever enough or perverse enough, and have enough selected facts to hand, you can make out convincing arguments to show that either everything is due to nature or everything is due to nurture! At the moment, the media are all climbing aboard the genetic (nature) bandwagon, but that will not last.

From the research so far undertaken on this subject it is clear that some very important aspects of what we call personality, and some very important *tendencies* we possess, are transmitted through the genes and can be said to be strongly connected to certain physical characteristics. One aspect of personality that is thought to be 'passed down' or 'inherited' in this way is the degree of *extrovert* or *introvert* behaviour. By extrovert behaviour is meant a kind of 'out-ward-focused' behaviour, so the extrovert is said to be a person who is highly sociable and interested in physical activities, often described as the life and soul of the party. Introvert behaviour, on the other hand, is 'inward-focused' behaviour, so that the introvert is described as a quiet person, uncomfortable with too many people around, inclined to be inward-looking, given to reflection, and more focused on their own thoughts and feelings than on so-called outgoing activities. These tendencies, i.e. to be a certain mixture of outward-lookingness and inward-lookingness, are said to be genetically based, and so are certain other characteristics.

But hold on! Does that mean God just *made* me as I am with every bit of behaviour already built in at birth? Has God made some of us with inherited criminal characteristics, and some of us with inherited rapist characteristics? And am I an anxious person, or a hard person, or a sad person, simply because – like extroversion and introversion – it's built into me – like a puppet or wind-up toy?

No, it does not mean that. We are overlooking what we said earlier about the other aspect of personality and development – the learning process. A great deal of what we loosely call our personality has developed as a result of the learning process, which of course extends far beyond formal (school and college) education, and started from day one of our lives, or even earlier, and involves our parents and other care-givers, and the kind of society and culture into which we are born or into which we move. Mark's conviction that everything was *his* fault was not a conviction he was born with, even if (and it may be quite a big *if*) he was born with a genetic tendency to be easily influenced.

In fact, some psychologists (but not all, since we ourselves are still groping for knowledge) like to use the term 'tempera-ment' to refer to traits or characteristics with a physical (genetic) basis, and the term 'personality' for the complete set of behaviours that make up any individual. So the term 'person-ality' would *include* temperament, and temperament is then seen as the physical contribution to the complete personality.

Before discussing a few aspects of Mark's life experiences we need to get it clear that his statement, 'I seem to have been born that way', was not strictly true, and as for changing his behaviour and his belief systems about his self, let's remind ourselves of two biblical characters whose beliefs and behaviour (and personalities) changed even though their genetic inheritance presumably remained the same.

Paul, or Saul as he was first called, had a set of beliefs or ideas that before his conversion, led him to behave as a persecutor. So in Acts we find: 'Meanwhile, Saul was still breathing out murderous threats against the Lord's disciples' (Acts 9.1). Here was the arch-persecutor demanding letters of authority to go and arrest and imprison people. What if Paul had said, 'I suppose that's what I was born with – I can't help it, I'm made like that'! But a great truth (*the* truth) was made known to Paul so that he became the person who could say: 'I have worked much harder, been in prison more frequently, been flogged more severely [than those criticizing him] and been exposed to death again and again. Five times I received from the Jews the forty lashes minus one . . . I have laboured and toiled and have often gone without sleep; I have known hunger and thirst . . . I have been cold and naked' (2 Corinthians 11.23–7).

What a change in outlook and behaviour!

In the disciple Peter we can perhaps see an even clearer example of a man who remained what he always seems to have been, an outgoing, rather impulsive extrovert, but who nevertheless changed in terms of behaviour, purpose and motivation. Here we see the impulsive 'big fisherman' who had denied Christ because he was afraid (as we would have been) turning into the, still extrovert, evangelist, but now instead of denial there was courage enough to amaze the rulers and elders: 'When they saw the courage of Peter and John and realised that they were unschooled, ordinary men, they were astonished and took note that these men had been with Jesus' (Acts 4.13).

Supposing Peter had believed, and gone on believing, that he was *born* timid, or that because of his inferior social position ('unschooled' or uneducated) he was a hopeless person, not suited at all to becoming a preacher! The things they said about him may have been 'true' (he was, in the eyes of the world, 'unschooled', and we know he lied out of fear when first accused of being an associate of Jesus), but he could and did become a different person while remaining essentially the *same* person. And this is possible for anyone reading these words.

Yes, Peter and Paul did have 'special' experiences and as Christians we may believe that they were changed at a deep spiritual level, and experienced spiritual rebirth, but they also boasted a whole new set of beliefs, a whole new set of attitudes. Never, as Mark did (p. 70), think that hopelessness is 'in the blood' (born that way, etc.); none of us needs to be trapped in that way of thinking. Our personal histories are important, but we are all individually responsible and change-able so far as our lives are concerned.

To experience in a chronic form feelings of inferiority, or to feel always that you are being assessed and found wanting, does not mean you have been severely repressed or abused in childhood. With some people, temperament, a fastidious upbringing, or what we may see as a 'correct' upbringing, could play a part in causing them to over-concentrate, over-focus, on behaviour, etiquette, class or other hierarchical structures and to feel ill at ease.

'What will people *think* of you' is one method of training and controlling children. 'People are *looking* at you' is another. Being looked at here means being looked at with disapproval or even disgust. The same parent who uses this 'being looked at' tactic to train the child is often the parent who desires the same child to be looked at as the star performer in the school play or on speech day. Of course we do have to train children in manners and other behaviour, so I am not intending to admon-ish parents – only to point out that even ordinary, acceptable treatment by loving parents may still affect a shy child in such a way that s/he becomes a shy adult. Some people begin to become over-conscious of their own performance: 'Am I doing it right?' or 'They'll think I'm stupid', etc. Unfortunately people with a tendency to shyness or to feeling inferior begin to see themselves in a negative light if given unhelpful 'messages'. They are forever assessing and damning themselves. They begin to get confused or flustered and may end up looking just the way they longed so much to avoid. Shyness and social-acceptance anxiety are self-replicating.

But bear in mind that the learning process (see Chapter One) has been involved here. It is possible, though, to *unlearn* and begin again. There is a process known as 'faulty thinking', and some people do a lot of faulty thinking about themselves, other people, and what they imagine other people *think* about them. Mark was one such person. Mark, however, did have some very serious self-deprecating experiences, which can be seen to have added enormously to any inclination he may have had towards easily imagining faults in himself.

For the first five years of Mark's life his father was a sergeant in the RAF, and saw his son only occasionally when on leave. Mark grew increasingly anxious about these occasions, and as the date of his dad's next leave drew near he would start wetting his bed. Dad was over-strict; he was severe. Mark could recall no memories involving his dad loving, cuddling or romping with him. Life became far worse after the age of five when his embittered father was discharged from the RAF owing to government cuts. Dad clearly decided not only to 'bring the lad up the right way' (i.e. to be tough and macho), but also to take it out on the child as a means of expressing his smouldering anger.

'I used to feel I was under a microscope all the time,' said Mark, 'or that I was being crushed by the strength of Dad's personality, and even now I can't stand up to him.'

Mark was a sensitive child who loved music and poetry, both interests that were sneered at by his father. But nearby lived a man who encouraged Mark in his music. From the age of eight, this friend allowed Mark to use his piano. Sadly, from the time Mark was about nine his musical 'friend' began to sexually abuse him, and this went on until Mark was nearly 15.

Mark's so-called friend used enticement (the music, the piano, and 'affection') to keep an emotional hold over him. It was easy to keep an emotional, almost blackmailing, hold over a child who received little or no affection from any other person.

'But I felt more and more worthless,' said Mark, 'and I also felt very guilty and confused. I felt I was the guilty one, not my friend. I felt more and more that people were looking at me and could tell things about me, and although I *know* it's stupid, this feeling has stayed with me, especially where women are concerned. When I talk to a woman I feel she knows this about me.'

Notice the 'faulty thinking' here. Poor Mark *felt* people were looking at him and *thinking* something bad about him. But if I, as a therapist, asked Mark what real evidence he had for this, what indicators there were to show that people had such thoughts, he could produce nothing; nothing apart from his own imagination. Admitting this, though, did not help him to stop the negative thoughts; they would not go away. 'I felt', said Mark, 'like I was being pursued by some kind of devil.'

Many people think like that. They feel helpless. They *always* switch over to a negative outlook whenever something happens that causes them the slightest concern. If, for example, a friend passes them in the High Street and appears not to notice them, they immediately come up with negative reasons to explain their friend's behaviour. Instead of thinking that the friend may have been preoccupied with some trouble or just daydreaming (both far more likely), they at once assume that the friend's behaviour meant that s/he was annoyed with them. From this thought they move on to examine what they themselves could have done to be so cast out by the friend, and they usually come up with quite a few possible flaws in their own recent behaviour.

To go back to the learning process, it is possible to say people learn this kind of behaviour; they form the habit of always being in the wrong, always being at fault, and always experiencing other people as judging them negatively. However, there are many psychotherapy and counselling approaches that enable people to either overcome, or at least drastically reduce, this negative behaviour and faulty thinking.

Mark's mother was a depressive. Depression in parents – and especially in mothers – may have an adverse effect on children. There is a lot of research evidence to back this up. I am not talking here of the occasional attack of 'the blues', times when Mum may feel a bit fed up and overwhelmed. I am talking of a deeper clinical depression, perhaps long-lasting or frequently recurring, where a mother can lose all interest in her child. How would Mark, as a three-year-old or a five-year-old, have experienced his mother's behaviour? He could not have said to himself, 'She's depressed, so it's understandable.' In fact, he would not have understood her moods at all. Although he would not have been able to verbalize on such matters, his *feelings* may have signalled to him such messages as, 'I am not liked . . . I am not nice, so I'm not liked.'

Mark as a young child probably used few words concerning his feelings, even to himself, but he learnt that if he reached out, as a child should do, to gain his mother's attention she showed a kind of hurtful behaviour – which, as a grown up, he could call *rejection*. Notice the way his thinking about himself in relation to others is being formed, trained, in childhood, and to *some* extent fixed – but only to some extent. With help he could unfix that way of thinking and feeling. Notice also that his mother needed help.

As an adult, Mark was using a metaphorical map to find his way through life, but his map was full of errors. If you are travelling and using a map, you are likely to get lost if the map is totally incorrect. Suppose, for the sake of argument, the important towns and cities were all in the wrong places, and the roads and motorways were equally incorrect. Anyone relying on this map would not only go astray, but would have an incorrect picture of what was out there! Many people have a totally incorrect social or psycho-social 'map' and this is what they use for their journey through life. In fact, none of our personal maps is completely correct.

Mark's map was well out. For example, that bit in his presenting problem: 'When . . . people decide to cancel dates with me, or worse, just not turn up . . . it must be my fault.' His map always told him it was his fault (echoes of his childhood?). But, time after time, when we examined situations he described and checked back on them, not only was there no evidence for this thinking, but also time and again those who were supposed to have shunned him were surprised to find that Mark had entertained such negative thoughts. Gradually, over many months, Mark became less likely to switch to 'negative' whenever he felt uncomfortable about some social interaction, and those uncomfortable feelings became infrequent. Mark's old map had given him what he thought was a correct picture concerning how to be accepted as a person. In some places his map told him that he must be seen as 'slick, even tough'. In the end he discovered that this was not necessary and that it did not suit his personality.

So many people are using psycho-social maps that are leading them astray in their thinking. All those worrying thoughts about what other people think about us; all those thoughts about how strong and confident *they* are; all those thoughts about other people's motives, thoughts that keep us awake at night, may be due to the use of an incorrect map.

Jesus' disciples probably had faulty 'maps' before his resurrection – except perhaps Peter. Jesus tests them out at one point and even reveals to Peter (then called Simon) that his *correct* perception had come from God. Jesus had been questioning the disciples concerning what people were saying about him: 'Who do people say the Son of Man is?' His disciples told him of the various ideas circulating, then Jesus presses further: '"But what about you?" he asked. "Who do you say I am?" Simon Peter answered, "You are the Christ, the Son of the living God." Jesus replied, "Blessed are you, Simon son of Jonah, for this was not revealed to you by man, but by my Father in heaven"' (Matthew 16.15–17).

Of course, as Christians our 'maps' should include our ideas and beliefs about what the Bible tells us. If the maps are wrong, and they may still be wrong even when we are Christians, we may experience conflict. There was conflict in Mark's life. On the one hand he had a map, his old map, telling him to be 'slick and even tough', but then he had a Bible 'map' that he thought was telling him to be 'meek and mild'. What did that mean?

Let's have a look and see how it may be possible to get errors appearing in our maps even where Christian ideas are concerned. First, where does the instruction come from to be 'meek and mild'? Most people come up with a message from Matthew's Gospel, chapter five, verse five, which says: 'Blessed are the meek, for they will inherit the earth'. So there! The Bible says 'be meek'.

But wait. By *meek* these days we mean sloppy, insipid, and almost spineless. Is that what Jesus meant? Words have a way of changing their meaning over time, and when translated into other languages (as Jesus' words have been) the meaning may be changed completely. If Jesus wanted his followers to be weak and spineless they certainly let him down. His immediate followers were anything but weak. They were prepared to suffer stoning and imprisonment and cruel deaths, not out of weakness but from strength and determination that were given to them by God. Stephen was strong enough in the Holy Spirit to call out to God as he was being killed by the stones: 'Lord, do not hold this sin against them' (Acts 7.60). How many of us would be strong enough to die under torture rather than betray our Lord?

One Bible commentator, William Barclay, points out that the Greek word *proates*, used in the Bible for what we have called 'meekness', actually refers to a strong, *balanced* characteristic, a happy medium between too much anger and too little anger, and this is the way he paraphrased Jesus' remarks in the 'sermon on the mount': 'O the bliss of the man who is always angry at the right time and never angry at the wrong time, who has every instinct, and impulse, and passion under control because he himself is God controlled, who has the humility to realize his own ignorance and his own weakness, for such a man is a King among men' (Barclay, 1975).

We can see, therefore, that if Mark thought that the Bible was telling him to be spineless and insipid (meek and mild), then his map was wrong again, and perhaps he *could* have benefited from some assertiveness training. To be assertive does not mean to be aggressive or arrogant. Jesus and his followers, people like St Paul, were certainly assertive – they could speak out boldly – but they were not aggressive or arrogant. Here is what Dr John Lockley has to say on that matter: 'It is easy to get depressed with the frustration of being unable to change events around you. Yet there *are* things you can do – lots of them. The whole topic of "making things happen" and "changing things" goes under the heading of Assertiveness Training. Unfortunately Christians often feel that they should not be assertive, but this is to misunderstand Christian doctrine' (Lockley, 1991).

Do not be afraid, even if you are a prayerful person, to seek the help of a professional psychotherapist or counsellor in order to get help in correcting some of the incorrect maps you may be carrying. Of course, when it comes to understanding the Bible you should seek the help of a Christian minister or counsellor. And remember, that awful shyness, those deep feelings of inferiority, those misinterpretations of other people's motives, can be replaced by comfortable feelings and a clearer picture of you and of other people. God wants you to live with your eyes open, both to the world and to him.

Compulsive obsessional thoughts

Marilyn's presenting problems

'At last,' sighed Marilyn on her first appointment, 'at last I've got round to talking about something that sounds so stupid I dared not tell anyone before. You see, I keep getting these terrible thoughts. I'm worried even about coming to you because I feel you'll do the same as I imagine others would – laugh at me!

'These thoughts keep bugging me and they won't leave me alone. And that sounds crazy because if they're *my* thoughts I needn't think them.'

Marilyn went on with some difficulty, 'The worst thing about it is that I'm supposed to be a Christian; I mean I actually go to Bible classes and all that. But as soon as I've got rid of one shocking thought another one comes along – sometimes I think I'm possessed!

'I really adore my husband and two young children, but yesterday, just to give you an example, while I was sharpening the carving knife I suddenly thought that I *might* cut their throats. I could do it while they were asleep.' Marilyn was trembling and on the verge of tears. 'And yet,' she continued, 'I *know* I wouldn't do that, if you can understand me. It sounds stupid, I know. I *know* I wouldn't, but I think I might! There was a murder done a few months ago near where I live, and I still sometimes feel I might have done it. No one knows how awful I feel, or how alone I feel, because I dare not tell anyone. I've not even told my parents or my husband. I'm even losing sleep now because I've started thinking I might commit a crime while sleep-walking.'

You will remember that when we discussed Anne's case in Chapter Two I named a number of what we call irrational fears, which were attached to objects such as spiders, or to social situations such as parties. These were called phobias. We are now, when we listen to Marilyn's story, hearing about a different sort of fear, or rather fear attached to thoughts, compulsive thoughts, or *compulsive obsessional* thoughts. Sometimes other names are used, such as 'phobia anxiety' or 'ruminative phobias'. In extreme cases, and Marilyn's was extreme, these thoughts, from which there seems to be no escape, can be socially, psychologically and even physically harmful. Psychiatrists and other therapists call the extreme condition an *obsessive compulsive disorder* (OCD), but there are many degrees of this troublesome way of thinking – ranging all the way from the childhood idea of some imminent danger from treading on the cracks in the pavement (and how many of us experienced that!) to full OCD. So lots of 'normal' folk experience these thoughts to some degree or other.

The term 'obsessive compulsive disorder' includes two recognizable experiences (or symptoms), although quite often the two are linked. There is, as I have said, the compulsive *idea* about what one may do or supposedly already has done. Ideas that inform you that you could be a murderer, or ideas that tell you that some evil or mishap will befall you or your family if, for example, you drive past a certain spot. These ideas can exist in the sufferer's mind without causing them to behave in a specific manner. This was Marilyn's sort of OCD.

The other form of OCD is directly attached to very specific *behaviour,* such as compulsive hand-washing, or compulsive mannerisms connected with ordinary procedures like walking through a doorway and feeling compelled to touch both door-posts as you do so, and having to go back out again and re-enter if you failed to do so. Some people with OCD say that if they are interrupted during any procedure or task, such as playing a piece of music, they *have to* start all over again from the beginning.

Many of us experience such compulsions to a mild degree – so no need to panic! But with some people they reach an extreme point and the person's whole lifestyle is affected, even leading to marital breakdown or loss of job. Yet practically all sufferers can be helped, some to the complete disappearance of the symptoms, many more to a tolerable state – almost down to what we might call 'normal' (or usual!).

To go back to Marilyn's problems, we can feel for her. She felt so alone. Then, as often happens, wrong ideas sometimes creep in. She said she sometimes believed she might be 'possessed'. Perhaps in her case this was only a remark that she did not intend her therapist to take seriously. There were certainly no grounds for such an idea. As a matter of fact, some of the most staunch Christians, including John Bunyan, the author of the *Pilgrim's Progress*, and Martin Luther seem to have suffered from some degree of OCD. Bunyan got the idea that he might suddenly say something awful in the middle of a sermon. In his book *Grace Abounding* he wrote:

> I could not tell how to speak my words for fear I should misplace them. Oh, how cautiously did I then go in all I did or said! I found myself as in a miry bog that shook if I did but stir . . . Whole floods of blasphemies were poured upon my spirit to my great Confusion and Astonishment . . . Instead of lauding and magnifying God the Lord, if I had but heard him spoken of, presently some horrible blasphemous thought or other would bolt out of my heart against him. (Rapoport, 1990)

God was still able to use people such as Bunyan and Luther in extraordinary ways, but it does not follow that he wants Christians or anyone else to torture themselves with such obsessional thoughts. Perhaps the most important words spoken by Marilyn, recorded in her first interview, are the words 'At last!' She came, at last, and received so much help that she now wonders how it was she could think and feel as she did. But she also knows that her silent prayers to God were answered in this special way. The author of the book *Miracles Happen When You Pray*, wrote: 'When we are dealing with an intractable problem in our hearts, it's a good time to realize that only God's spirit can shape us and make us into men and women who are both healed and holy. All we have to do is invite him to do so' (Sherrer, 1997).

Chronic anxiety and difficulties in decision-making

Janice's presenting problems

'As far back as I can remember I have been really scared about having to make any decisions. Of course, when I was a child all important decisions were made for me, but now I lie awake at night worrying about decisions I have to make the next day.

'It's not only about big important things either; I take hours to decide about anything. Even if I go to buy some shoes I may visit five shops and have a panic in each one, and in the end go home without buying any.

'Even going out brings on a panic because I have to decide what clothes to wear, and the worst part of all this is that when I have made a choice I then always feel I've made the wrong one. It seems as if I'm never free from worry. I have perhaps half a day when I feel clear; it's almost like I've forgotten to feel anxious, and then I'll find myself worrying about something else, something totally different to my last worry. But there are some things I worry about that keep coming round in turns, the same things week after week, month after month.'

Most of us will sympathize with Janice because to a certain extent we know only too well what she is talking about – if not concerning decision-making, then with worries that seem to live with us all the time. Certainly Janice's symptoms seem to be rather more intensive than most people will have experienced, but we can classify anxiety states all the way from 'normal' to 'pathogenic'.

In fact, Janice had two major problems: one was the problem of decision-making, and the other was this recurrent, chronic anxiety. Although both these states may merge into and affect each other, I shall look first at her decision-making problem, but before that here is something more about Janice's background and childhood.

Unlike many of the other cases I have discussed, as far as anyone could discover there was no dramatic evidence for the cause of Janice's problems, no parental rejection or abuse, no trauma-producing experiences, and no deserting parents. Moreover, with the problems I am discussing in this section, that seems frequently to be the situation. It is important to say this because we need to avoid the impression that anxiety, depression and panic states are all caused by poor parenting and unhappy childhoods, or even by some organic lesion or malfunction. Most of the conditions I am discussing may be experienced by people who have lived ordinary lives in ordinary families.

Janice was a doctorate (PhD) student interested in archae-ology, so I can at once dispel the delusion some people seem to entertain when they express the opinion that this inability to make decisions is associated with a low intelligence rating. No doubt the problem exists in the case of some people with learning difficulties, but it seems that some quite 'brainy' people are also affected.

Janice was an only child, who had fond, supportive parents. Although her upbringing (social training, social skills, etc.) was not rigid or strict, she did receive fairly clear messages regarding how to behave, what was 'nice' and 'not nice', and what was acceptable and unacceptable behaviour. If we are bent on looking for causes we might begin to make a link between Janice's temperament and genes (see Mark's case) and these clear, strong messages she received from society and parents from babyhood upwards. Maybe, we could argue, her tempera-ment was such that even normal guidance caused her to become over-concerned as a child with 'right' and 'wrong', 'good' and 'bad', and so forth. *Maybe*, but this has to remain speculative.

One thing was certain, and Janice clearly said so; she lacked confidence in some areas of her life. While being intellectually rigorous and precise, she flopped when it came to what she called 'ordinary living', and along with this went a strong tendency towards faulty thinking (see Mark's case).

People like Janice live with fears. I said at the start of this book that fear would be an ingredient in many of the difficulties discussed in these pages. It is not so much the common fears about being molested or having an operation, nor is it the fear found in those obsessional phobic states (fear of heights, of spiders, of confined spaces, etc.). Instead, it is a fear of being judged by others and found wanting. In fact, it can also be a fear of self-judgement and self-condemnation. Behind much of the fear we can hear the condemnatory question, 'What will people think of you?' These people worry so much over what others will think of them if they do or say anything 'wrong', or if they even make a wrong choice. Any failure to come up to the (often high) standard the sufferer sets for herself or himself will be experienced as some kind of disgrace.

But worse, catastrophe might follow – that is to say, events that people like Janice would *imagine* as leading to catastrophe. What if she chose the wrong pair of shoes! Then, she told herself, her friends, or her mother, or her boyfriend would dislike them and imply that once again she'd chosen wrongly. All this thinking, based entirely on her own imagination and not on anything anyone had said, would convince Janice that she was hopeless. At such a point Janice would hurriedly leave the shop, her heart racing, her temperature rising – and no new shoes! And, of course, as far as Janice was concerned she would have confirmed as true those things she said about herself: 'I'm hopeless at making decisions, I always get scared.'

When reading this you will appreciate that perhaps because of her 'nervous temperament' (in popular language) Janice's mind and body would seem to have formed certain habitual ways of thinking and responding. In other words, she had *learnt* to think and respond in these ways and to believe that whatever choice she made, whatever decision she came to, the result would be a catastrophe. Janice was not mad, she was not crazy, she did not need hospital treatment, but she needed help in sorting out her beliefs, her perspectives, her ideas about what was important and what didn't really matter all that much.

Now let's consider Janice's other major problems. She said, in her first session: 'But there are some things I worry about that keep coming round in turns, the same things week after week, month after month.' This sort of anxiety is often called *free-floating anxiety*. Millions of people experience free-floating anxiety, and during therapy they often come up with some interesting ways of describing it. One man said it reminded him of trying to have a picnic in a meadow swarming with flies or wasps. As soon as the fly is shoo-ed off the pork pie, it settles on the sherry trifle, and it may repeat this annoying behaviour time and time again.

Like so many anxiety or phobic states, free-floating anxiety may be only mildly troublesome, something a group of friends may joke about, or it may convey experiences too horrible to be reduced to the level of humour. That, in fact, goes for anxiety in general. We can smile, for example, when we read the letter, written as a class exercise in school, by a boy called Mike. The children had been asked to write a letter to God. Mike wrote, 'Dear God, What is it like when you die. Nobody will tell me, I just want to know, I don't want to do it. Your friend, Mike.' There was just a little bit of anxiety as well as curiosity showing through in that letter (Marshall and Hample, 1967).

But free-floating anxiety can be so terribly tiring. It can exhaust people; it can wear them down physically as well as emotionally, and it may make some people feel depressed, yet it is so, so common. At the start of this book I asked, 'How is it that when you've got "everything" – good health, good job, friends, family, etc. – one scary feeling after another looms up?' Especially, we may ask, why does this happen with Christians? True, some believers have been helped by the comforting and strengthening words to be found in the Bible and in hymns, or those spoken by a Christian minister or friend. It may be helpful to remind ourselves of some of the former now.

Here's a verse from the hymn 'Father, I place into your hands':

> Father, I place into your hands
>   My friends and family.
> Father, I place into your hands
>   The things that trouble me.
> Father, I place into your hands
>   The person I would be,
> For I know I can always trust in you.

Say those last words again: 'For I know I can always trust in you'. And so many of us mean it; *intellectually* we know that we can trust God. Peter stepped out of the boat, but Jesus had to rescue him. Was that the end of it for Peter? Of course not. Yet we go on worrying, and we may even get to worrying about worrying! Have you ever thought that, so far as human achievement is concerned, God may actually invite you to feel 'free to fail'? Suppose *this* happens, suppose *that* happens, we say, suppose I *fail*? So what? Russ Parker wrote a book called *Free to Fail*, and another author writing about the book said: 'It helped me to realize that many of the prophets in the Bible were called to tasks for which the result would be failure, for example Jeremiah failed to turn his people away from their sin, and suffered terribly himself. When Isaiah was called (in Isaiah 6) he responded, but was told that his people would take no notice of his message' (Young, 2000).

Many actions are failures in human terms. No doubt many onlookers felt Stephen had failed in his mission as he was stoned to death. Yet such deaths as Stephen's helped to spread the gospel across the world. Remember, therefore, that whatever you do, in prayer and with love in your heart, need not cause you anxiety: 'The Lord is near. Do not be anxious about anything, but in everything, by prayer and petition, with thanksgiving, present your requests to God' (Philippians 4.5–6).

Some people, though – like Janice – remain very distressed because of this awful cloud of worry, which moves from subject to subject in their mind. Here are some diary notes kept by 'Mrs X'. This lady would spend days struggling with one subject on which anxiety had settled. That subject would then take a back seat for a while, while Mrs X's anxiety would promptly alight on another of her favourite anxiety subjects:

1 Slight pain in left breast. Convinced I'm getting cancer (5 days of worry)

2 Have I upset my friend, Jackie? (3 days of worry, one overlapping with 1 above)

3 My husband's cough – tuberculosis or lung cancer (2 weeks of worry with overlap)

4 Child, Mandy, to have triple vaccination for measles, mumps and rubella. She might become autistic! Or worse! (A week's worry this time, but I can see this anxiety coming round often)

5 Awoke to find my left ear hearing less than the right ear – going deaf! (4 days' worry with overlap to 4 above)

6 There's that pain again in left breast – definitely breast cancer! (Worried, on and off, for 9 weeks. Couldn't sleep either. All tests negative. Nothing wrong with left breast)

7 Guilt worry: I won't go to heaven when I die. I obviously don't trust God (3 days' intense worry)

8 Worry about humans becoming more evil. Worry started when I saw news bulletin; terrorists shot 16 tourists dead (worry spread over 14 days overlapping with 6 and 7 above)

9 Yesterday felt grand – no worry, felt free as a bird – now worry about feeling free from worry.

And on and on it goes. Keeping people awake at nights, causing them to avoid some special gatherings, even family gatherings, never having so much as ten days free from anxiety. Now let's be clear, a certain degree of anxiety or concern is necessary and even good. We do need to be aware of life's real dangers. People need to look ahead and to become concerned if children or young people could be taking a wrong or dangerous path, metaphorically or literally. That is not the same thing as we saw in Mrs X's diary notes. But even if you are a Mrs X or a Mr X you still may be able to cope because the things you worry about are in some ways shallow and you *know* it, and it does not hinder you much. Plenty of folk go through life like that.

But if anxiety leads on to depression, or causes you to become physically affected in some way, such as severe and chronic headaches, or chronic intestinal pains, first see your GP and check out that these pains are the result of chronic severe anxiety, and if so seek the help of a psychotherapist or counsellor, and of course make sure s/he is well qualified. That is what Janice did.

Before closing this section, however, I want to remind readers that some people have very real, and often lonely, anxiety about deep and important matters to do with their *beliefs*. We have all met people who were 'screwed up' because they no longer felt they could hold to the faith in which they were brought up. Yet they could not talk to those around them about these deep and troublesome, even painful, spiritual experiences. Sometimes these *existential* worries, as we call them, can lead to depression, and those with these sort of doubts are not always encouraged to talk about such feelings. It is surely wrong that such sufferers, for they do suffer, should be told that seeing a counsellor is not acceptable for a Christian, or that they should be offered drug therapy only, even though that too may help them.

During the writing of this part of the book, the terrible events of 11 September 2001 took place. These events caused many people to feel a sense of shock and depression. Some of these people found themselves worrying about the world and even, perhaps for the first time, they began to worry about 'what life is about', or 'why are we so evil?' and many other existential matters. Christian ministers, Christian counsellors and psychotherapists may all be used by God where people feel they have a burden and want to talk.

Janice had much to unlearn, and much to learn, despite her academic abilities. It took her many months, nearly two years in fact, to do this and to reach a stage when she felt comfortable. She was beginning to find peace. In a little booklet called

A *Mind at Ease*, Dr Marion Ashton wrote concerning Christ:
'He suffered pressure from foes, pressure from friends, pressure
from circumstances, pressure from Satan, physical, mental, and
spiritual pressure; and yet through it all He had such peace
that when we read His words, "Peace I leave with you, My
peace I give unto you" our hearts know that, that is the very
kind of peace we want, His peace' (Ashton, 1987).

Problems in controlling anger, and the search for meaning

Bill's presenting problems

'I am a social worker, and I might as well tell you that
I am just about fed up with social work and all that goes
along with it. Actually I'm not doing the kind of work
I really like doing, the sort of work that first attracted
me into social work. I'm what they call a "regional
officer" now, which means I'm the senior worker, the
boss if you like, for a biggish area with a population of
350,000 covered by five area teams of social workers.

'However, the main reason for coming for help is
my temper. I can't control it – which is a pretty poor
advert for a social worker. I've always been a bit quick
off the mark; short fuse as they say, but I'm getting
worse. In fact twice in the last year my wife has left me
for her own safety.

'By the way, my wife's a Christian; I don't know
why I told you that, except that when we first met I
thought I was one too. That's all gone out of the
window as far as I'm concerned. I think the rot set in
when I went to college and did sociology and all that.
Life's got no meaning now.'

Bill's voice drifted to a stop, as a sort of reflective
expression took hold. 'Yes,' he said in answer to a
question, 'I'm on tranquillizers.' He named a benzo-
diazepine-based drug.

Bill sounded like a man who had lost his way, and lost much of the joy of life. As in some other cases I've reported, marital breakdown seemed imminent. Twice recently his wife had left home. Even in this brief statement, telling me why he had come for help, this intelligent and hard-working man had given a pen-picture of a gradual slide downwards from a time when he enjoyed his work, was happy in his marriage, and life still had some meaning.

Let's look a little closer at the facts surrounding his downward drift – a drift not only in his beliefs, but in his health. Bill arrives for therapy as an unhappy person, and a person depending to some extent on benzodiazepine drugs. One of the first things to notice is that outwardly, to the world at large, he has 'progressed' – that is to say, he has become a 'successful' regional officer in a large social services department. But now he has less rather than more control over his temper, and it is getting worse. Further, his attitude to life has changed; 'Life's got no meaning now'. He has achieved promotion, but it has not brought happiness. It has not even brought security so far as his marriage is concerned.

There are three ingredients here – *at least* three, possibly more. The first is stress. Bill was a man experiencing stress at work. The stress at work helped to produce stress at home. He had not recently arrived at a stressful work situation – he had been under stress right from his first appointment as a social worker, but the stress factor had increased with each promotional step.

Secondly, there was his basic temperament. 'I've always been a bit quick off the mark', he had said, but in reality at the time we first met he was dangerously near to being charged with the offence of grievous bodily harm. At work it was only verbal explosions that occurred, but at home and in other situations, if frustrated, he might throw a full mug of coffee across the room, or smash a window out with his fist, or hit his wife across the face.

The third ingredient in Bill's unhappy state was what I am calling his 'existential' problem. His meaning of life problem.

He was not simply making a wry comment when he said that life now had no meaning for him. He was actually troubled in his mind. He was having worrying thoughts concerning religion, rationalism, atheism and humanism – lots of 'isms' in fact. His wife's struggle to live according to her Christian faith only frustrated and irritated Bill all the more. So here we have stress, temperament and existential (spiritual) problems. I shall consider these aspects separately, although in fact they were intertwined in Bill's life.

First, stress. As a subject of study it is not a simple subject, but it is interesting and important. Did you know that some things might be stressing you without you realizing it? Did you know that as a result of prolonged stress, harmful changes might take place in your body? An interesting experiment was carried out by two researchers some years ago, which showed that people can be stressed even when they are unaware of the stress-producing factor:

> 'A study by Lazarus and McClaery . . . involved showing subjects particular words on a screen and then with some of the words giving them an electric shock. Other words were neutral and did not accompany a shock at all. Not surprisingly the subjects in this study developed a reaction, through classical conditioning, to those words which had been accompanied by shock, and when they saw them again (without an electric shock) they produced a strong GSR response (i.e. skin changes which could be measured). But the interesting thing which Lazarus and McCleary discovered was that when they presented the words subliminally (i.e. so faintly and so quickly that the subjects were not aware of having seen anything at all) they still showed a strong GSR reaction. So we may be experiencing stress from something even though we do not realize it at the time' (Hayes and Orrell, 1987).

What about the other happening – changes going on inside us in chronic stress? So wonderful has God made the human body that it is equipped with its own pharmacy, its own drug store! And its own diagnostic computer systems for rapidly coming up with the right 'medicine' – the exact 'medicine' required to balance things out. Two of these marvellous systems are the endocrine and the immune systems, and in the main they work well together to cope with all manner of stress, as well as attacks on the body by germs, poisons and various foreign bodies. These systems can adjust the working of the body by switching chemicals (e.g. hormones) on and off as nature intended for short periods during stress, injury or illness. Unfortunately, modern-day living often subjects the human body to prolonged periods of stress (e.g. some types of stress at work), so that the chemicals are switched on or off for too long or short a period, thus damaging the body and its immune system.

When this happens we may get various physical symptoms ranging from mild, chronic abdominal pains to full-blown gastric ulcers. We may suffer from too many colds or sore throats. We may feel exhausted even after hours of sleep or become run down and short-tempered. But note what is happening: the prolonged stress (with anxiety and tension) is affecting the functioning of the endocrine, immune and nervous systems. Because this causes more minor illness, tiredness and irritability, the body now begins to affect the brain (or mind) so that we may feel depressed. Prolonged dysfunctional stress sets up a vicious circle.

I referred above to *dysfunctional* stress. Does this mean we can have *functional* stress? In other works, is there good and bad stress? Depending on our meaning of the word 'stress', the answer is yes; we can have good stress as well as bad. If the word 'stress' is restricted to uncomfortable stress, then of course there is only one kind – bad stress. But it seems we must have a wider definition, which may include 'demanding but interesting and absorbing' work, and engaging in activities such as sports, drama, solving puzzles and many other things that all call for heightened body/mind reactions.

Each of these activities may be defined as stressful in the sense of being 'demanding' to some extent. For many people, though, doing a stressful job that they thoroughly enjoy, or jumping from an aeroplane and free-floating for a few hundred yards, produces what we may call *good* stress. This is so especially when it is 'their thing', it is going well, and is not producing other stressful factors such as financial debt. Even going for a swim, or doing some other physical activity such as running, will subject the body to some stress, but after such an exercise we are likely to feel 'high' ('runners' high') rather than 'low'. If we had no stress at all, physical, intellectual, spiritual or functional, we'd all turn into rice puddings!

Most of Bill's stress, dysfunctional stress, seemed to come from the job he was doing – perhaps not social work itself, but the senior post of 'regional officer'. Before considering that further, though, let's look at that other ingredient: temperament.

Here was a man who had a dangerously short fuse and a violent temper. But could it be that sometimes the use of this sort of language, 'a short fuse', is merely an excuse, a way of hiding behind some factor over which we pretend we have no control? 'I can't help it – I'm made that way. I have a short fuse.'

Of course, Bill's temperament was an ingredient (so was St Paul's in his day, and look how he changed in behaviour and belief), and obviously the stress of the job was present for him, (although that is something else he could change – his job). But (see Chapter One) the 'learning process' was also involved. In Bill's case, as well as 'always' having been 'quick off the mark', he had come to believe (i.e. he had *learnt*) that to reveal any 'weakness' or to be discovered to have been 'wrong' in any respect was utterly disgraceful, bad, a failure. It took some time for him to appreciate, during therapy, how this had come about over the years since childhood, but the main effect was that any criticism or exposure of personal 'defects' or 'failings' was perceived by Bill as a threat to his ego. This defensiveness, combined with his basic temperament, *plus* the effects of stress, would cause the 'short fuse' display of bad temper. But the most telling ingredient was the demand for infallibility and the feeling of shame, producing rage, when he felt criticized or exposed.

Despite all I have said in this book about the effects of parenting, about attachment and the learning theory, I believe that people, adult individuals, must take responsibility for their own behaviour. OK, they may be helped to see things in a different way but, setting aside any philosophical discussions on free will versus determinism, the element of choice is still meaningful. Everyone has the gift of choice and, like Joshua, we too must choose: 'But if serving the LORD seems undesirable to you, then choose for yourselves this day whom you will serve . . . But as for me and my household, we will serve the LORD' (Joshua 24.15). Unlike Joshua, Bill was defending his violent actions by implying he had no choice – 'I'm made that way'.

Bill's response with anger, whenever he thought he was being criticized, was in truth the response of an emotionally immature person. Very young infants of two or three years of age have little control over their basic impulses so they hit out or throw themselves to the ground when frustrated. Bill, like many other adults, had not really learnt to control his impulses. It takes an emotionally mature person to calmly accept criticism.

Despite what we have said about anger, and anger itself not necessarily being bad or wicked, there are times when we must 'control our anger, our jealousy and our resentment as an act of self-denial as Christ works in us' (Shields and Bredfeldt, 2001). See also the epistle of James, 'Everyone should be quick to listen, slow to speak and slow to become angry' (James 1.19).

Having looked at Bill's stress experience and his temperament, or having considered these factors in a general way, we may be in a better position to consider more closely his job, and the subject of jobs and temperament in general. The Bible sometimes instructs that we *walk away* from certain situations. Much of our modern approach, however, seems to be concerned (even over-concerned) with forcing ourselves to adapt to ever increasing stress in unsuitable jobs. Can this always be the right philosophy? Have we gone too far with the notion that it is a failure on the part of the individual if he or she does not stick to a certain type of work, certain work situations, and does not aim constantly for promotion in a job that will inevitably bring added tension, ill health, and perhaps some kind of nervous breakdown?

Consider Bill's work history in this light. He said, 'Actually I'm not doing the kind of work I really like doing, the sort of work that first attracted me into social work.' True, and it is probably fair to say that he was not, as a regional officer, doing the sort of work that he was most suited to. The way things had developed and changed within state social service departments, and his promotions, meant that Bill now had to work along lines contrary to most of his personality traits. He had found it enjoyable, almost relaxing, to meet individuals with their personal problems, but as a regional officer his day was full of committee meetings, staff squabbles, staff training and the like. He found the stress and the tension of chairing committee meetings quite overwhelming. He could never sleep the night before one, so the tiredness the next day made his functioning even worse. Furthermore, as a senior officer he found himself obliged to propagate ways of economic management that he did not favour, and which he felt were harmful to the people he and his junior colleagues were supposed to be serving.

Yet of course Bill struggled on, as do millions of others. Changing jobs or giving up promotions, and the salary or wage increases that accompany promotions, are decisions that have to rest with the individuals concerned and their partners and families. Not everybody is able to consider changes of this sort. However, I can say that many who have done so, even when it meant living on a reduced salary, have found so much relief from stress, so much improvement in health, and so much more quality time with their families, that they have thanked God for the change. This subject, therefore, became a matter for discussion in Bill's therapy sessions.

He had a third problem area, though – his existential problems. By 'existential' I mean here the feeling, attitudes, beliefs and anxieties that have to do with the meaning and purpose of life, of existence, of *being*, and the 'why are we here?' questions. No other species on this planet is likely to experience existential thoughts. This is a human characteristic. Another of our case subjects, Janice – who you read about on page 84– struggled with existential problems.

Not everyone seems to be 'awakened' to this kind of thinking – although perhaps it is a matter of degree or the extent to which different people are awakened. Most folk think round these matters now and again, particularly during adolescence, but they usually end up with a few peripheral thoughts or clichés, or they dismiss such thinking as 'beyond me . . . does your head in, all that stuff!'

Other people find that existential questions do bother them. It is possible that many more people are affected by such matters, but neither they nor others recognize their problems as being existential. Some meet up with difficulties when they go on to higher education at college or university. Beliefs and value systems with which they had grown up are challenged, and they are forced to reflect on these values and beliefs. Others seem to meet with a challenge to their beliefs when something traumatic occurs in their lives. For a minority these existential aspects of life become the most vital and demanding aspects; they become *driven* to resolve apparent conflicts, or they find it imperative to search for meaning, or for a new meaning.

I believe that this existential factor represents a special human need, and I am not alone in believing this. So important is this area of human struggle that a special form of counselling called 'existential counselling' has developed. A leading practitioner states: 'People who come for counselling are often confused because they cannot make sense of life or some aspect of life. They are frequently struggling to accommodate two or more conflicting views of life. They may just have discovered that the ways in which they used to make sense of life are no longer valid in the face of a new development or crisis' (Deurzen-Smith, 1988, p. 3).

This seemed to have happened in Bill's case. As he put it, '. . . the rot set in when I went to college and did sociology and all that'. But don't let's blame sociology for Bill's existential problems; it was more complicated than that. When he went to college he really hadn't thought deeply at all about existence or the meaning of life. So the whole experience of examining, for the first time, his basic ideas and premises brought about the collapse of what was really a flimsy edifice, and he was able to put nothing of value in its place. In the therapy situation he was able to take a long cool look at the stress factors in his current life situation, as well as the behavioural and temperamental factors. He reassessed his future work role and aims, and he found that talking about those existential factors helped him to begin to redefine his own system of values. 'Best of all,' he said, 'me and Sue [his wife] have been able to spend hours talking about our beliefs. I know she prays for my conversion, as she puts it. Well, we'll see . . . !'

Stress, tension and irritable bowel syndrome (IBS)

Jonathan's presenting problems

At his initial meeting with me, Jonathan said, 'I get these awful gut pains here', and he lightly swirled his right hand over his abdomen. He continued, 'I've had them now, off and on, for about five years, but they've gradually got worse. That's why I saw my doctor. She couldn't find anything so she referred me to Mr Crowshaw at the infirmary – he's a gastroenterologist.' Jonathan then recited all the tests he'd had, and finished up saying '. . . so they all seem to think it's got something to do with stress, or worry.'

None of the doctors, including the specialist, could find anything 'wrong' with Johnathan's 'guts'. That is to say, they could find nothing *organically* wrong with his intestines. They could not find ulceration, nor cancerous cells, nor blockages, nothing that they could name as a lesion, yet there was still this pain. So the hospital consultant, the gastroenterologist, had recommended psychotherapy with a focus on relaxation and the reduction of stress.

I have already discussed various aspects of stress – for example, in relation to Bill. But here I want to stay with a particular health hazard that is often stress-related and was seen in Jonathan's case: *irritable bowel syndrome* (IBS).

It is becoming more usual to talk about IBS nowadays, but it is still not all that easy because so many people, especially the sufferers, find it embarrassing to speak about, and this of course made it more difficult for Jonathan. And it is a subject that easily lends itself to little smutty jokes or sniggers, and even to puns, some of which come out without intention – such as when someone says to an IBS patient, 'we must get to the bottom of this condition'. However, in reality the condition is not at all funny for IBS sufferers, some of whom cannot travel far or even go into town unless they know exactly how far away the nearest loo will be at any time. Nor is it all that amusing when you have to carry a card asking for a seat in the auditorium 'near the exit or toilet facility'.

Jonathan is a sales rep. In fact, he is the area sales representative for a firm that manufactures washing-machines. He claims to have experienced a happy childhood and to have been strongly encouraged by both his parents always to be honest, punctual, reliable and hard-working. What more could his employers wish for? Jonathan's mother died when he was 16 and although he had a good and hard-working father, Jonathan felt responsible for his ten-year-old sister and eight-year-old brother, and this concern for their welfare continued into their early adulthood. His family, as well as having a strong set of moral values, have always been regular church attenders.

Now, at 45, Jonathan feels decidedly burdened. His firm is in difficulty and the threat of redundancy looms over him. Actual internecine staff warfare over such matters as promotions keeps him awake night after night, and he is constantly haunted by, of all things, the value of the pound sterling, since that affects sales.

Although he and his wife, Stella, still have their marriage intact there are financial pressures and worries all round. Their son, aged 21, and daughter, aged 19, have both obtained university places, but this only adds to the financial strain. Over time, Jonathan and Stella have moved into a totally flat, neutral relationship, and without fully realizing it have gradually spent less and less time together, and even *less* time socializing. Gradually, all spiritual, and even emotional, involvement has deserted them, and along the same gradual track Jonathan's pains and exhaustion have increased.

In the United Kingdom, as we move apprehensively into the twenty-first century, it appears that 40 per cent of a family doctor's time is taken up with dealing with problems to do with anxiety, depression and stress; and stress caused by so many 'external' factors seems often to be linked to tension within the body. It is this tension that so often affects the body producing, among other symptoms, pain. We need to pause here and question again. Should it be the same for Christians? Family–work–stress–pain? Should there not be an inner peace, no matter what is happening in the world around us? Christ, though, did not promise an easy life that would be free from suffering. In fact, it is recorded that he said, 'I have told you these things, so that in me you may have peace. In this world you will have trouble. But take heart! I have overcome the world' (John 16.33). Is that statement true? If it is, and I believe it is, why do so many of us, ordained ministers included, experience illness resulting from tension and stress? Why haven't we taken Jesus' message to heart?

Well, for a start, we – and here the word 'we' refers to our society as a whole – are tending to cheat. We believe in God, fine. We believe in Jesus and the Holy Spirit, of course. So now we want the inner peace. But we have left out of the equation or the contract (or covenant) our own behaviour and the structure and quality of modern (or post-modern) Western society. All the way through the Bible we read of God telling humankind how they are to live and what sort of societies they should establish, and in St Paul's writings, as well as in the Gospels, we are likewise told how we should live, and love, and care for our brethren (the peoples of the world). Even when referring to the Holy Spirit, the New Testament links the blessings (e.g. the peace) with obedience to God's wishes: 'We are witnesses of these things, and so is the Holy Spirit, whom God has given *to those who obey him*' (Acts 5.32, my italics).

Just for a moment try standing back and viewing two aspects of life at the same time: our society and our individual selves. Our society will include our television programmes, our news media in general, the attitude of many people to getting rich quickly, the 'consumer society', the plight of starving children, war-torn lands, politics and societal greed. With all these and more in mind, beside our individual selves, consider these words from the New Testament: 'The acts of the sinful nature are obvious: sexual immorality, impurity and debauchery; idolatry and witchcraft, hatred, discord, jealousy, fits of rage, selfish ambition, dissensions, factions and envy; drunkenness, orgies and the like. I warn you, as I did before, that those who live like this will not inherit the Kingdom of God' (Galatians 5.19-20).

Life hasn't changed much, has it! How many of these behaviours were touching Jonathan and his family? True, debauchery was not directly involved, but discord, jealousy, selfish ambition, dissensions, factions and envy are all there in the work situation, and in society at large there is still immorality, idolatry (which can mean idolizing footballers or pop stars, or even material possessions), fits of rage – even road rage – and plenty of envy. There is also cheating and selfishness, much of it passed off as business or management skilfulness.

Of course, poor Jonathan cannot be blamed for this list of evils but, as I have pointed out elsewhere, we are all caught up in the sin that infects the societies of the world. Jonathan, in fact, was a very 'moral' man in that he was more honest, punctual, reliable and hard-working than most people. But therein lies the irony. It was partly *because* of his strong moral principles that Jonathan suffered more tension than his colleagues, many of whom were prepared to 'slack off' at work or be dishonest over 'trivial' matters such as punctuality or reliability, and generally to function at a lower, more comfortable, moral level.

So we can see an aspect of moral conflict gradually creeping into Jonathan's life. The 'world' would be saying 'slack off, mate' or 'shove in a bit of overtime when you didn't actually do it' or, higher up in the hierarchy, 'my expected bonus as chairman of the company is £3 million'. But Jonathan can hear his mother's voice going on about honesty and fairness or his father's voice advocating reliability and punctuality. Conflict!

So what has all this to do with Jonathan's presenting problem, his irritable bowel? And why should his doctor have sent him to see a psychotherapist? This sounds a bit like saying, 'It's all in the head, go and see a shrink', which people quite rightly get annoyed about. But the doctor knew very well that Jonathan's pain was not in the head, it was in his intestines. She also knew that damaging stress and prolonged anxiety could bring about various physical ailments – real ailments, not just imaginary ones. These ailments can include various skin diseases, stomach upsets and even stomach ulcers, itching (pruritis), and inflammation of various membranes (including of course those in the intestines), so it made sense for Jonathan to see a psychotherapist or counsellor. However, in the case of certain ailments and illnesses such as IBS – and for example anorexia nervosa – it is necessary that the therapist has received some special training in these conditions and knows how best to help the sufferer. After a couple of months of special treatment that included, as well as counselling, the use of imagery and relaxation techniques, Jonathan's pain level has fallen considerably and his spasmodic bouts of IBS have become less frequent. Above all, though, there is a different, happier life for him and Stella.

In discussing Jonathan's case I have centred on some very physical, 'medical', aspects. However, I have pointed out that these physical aspects were not unconnected with emotional aspects and conflict. More and more it becomes clear that healing has to do with the *whole* person – physical, social and spiritual. There were parts of Jonathan's case that would be the concern of a Christian pastor and adviser, but there were also clear medical aspects.

Christians should remember that the very best medicine must come from the feeling of joy in knowing, believing, and experiencing the reality of the living God in Jesus Christ. We have seen how fear, anxiety and stress can affect the body's systems negatively, but *real* joy also affects the body in a positive, health-preserving way. To feel that you really are in Christ, to live in him rather than just believe intellectually, can bring physical as well as spiritual health. St Paul writes: 'May the God of hope fill you with all joy and peace as you trust in him, so that you may overflow with hope by the power of the Holy Spirit' (Romans 15.13).

Four

Blessed assurance, Jesus is mine.

I shall start this chapter with four pen-pictures concerning work with children. Because they were children, they did not all arrive with clear statements that could be called 'presenting problems', although of course they did 'present with problems'. Unlike the phone-in or drop-in centres that children are encouraged to use these days, it is more usual in psychotherapy practices for children to be brought by parents or 'referred' by their GPs, although some children are referred by the social service departments.

Sensitive children

Dave's problems

Dave was referred by his GP, and his mother brought him to the centre. The reasons given for his referral, his 'presenting problems', were that he wet the bed nightly and had a bad stammer. Dave was ten years old when he was referred.

Both Dave's parents had full-time jobs. He had one sibling; an older sister who was 12. The family had a nice home; it was very comfortable with well-kept gardens. Dave, young as he was, had told his parents that he was a Christian and that he wanted to go to special meetings for 10–12-year-olds run by the local church.

So, on the face of it, there did not seem to be social reasons for Dave's stammering and bed-wetting. Perhaps, said some people, there were physical causes, something organically wrong. But this had been thoroughly checked out by doctors and the speech therapist, and nothing abnormal had been found.

At this point some might suggest intensive prayer to seek guidance concerning the origin of Dave's problems: 'Is any one of you in trouble? He should pray. Is anyone happy? Let him sing songs of praise. Is any one of you sick? He should call the elders of the church to pray over him and anoint him with oil in the name of the Lord' (James 5.13–14).

According to one reading of the Bible, though, it is seldom implied that we must *only pray* and never look around to see what else we may do in order to alter things – and maybe improve some of the conditions in the lives of others. No one can deny the *doing* aspect taught in the parable of the Good Samaritan. And since I have quoted from James on prayer, I cannot ignore some other words of the same writer when he said: 'Show me your faith without deeds, and I will show you my faith by what I do' (James 2.18).

Was there nothing needing to be changed in Dave's family, changes that God would wish to be made? Consider a few of the conditions experienced by Dave in his 'happy' family. How, for example, did he experience Dad? He loved both his parents but he nevertheless felt under great pressure from his father.

Dave's dad had always admired his own prowess as a sportsman. He declared that men should be *men,* which in his eyes meant they should be 'butch' and 'macho'. He was, he said, 'Disgusted – well, disappointed' over Dave. 'I've given up on him,' he said, 'tried to get him into football – hopeless! Now with his *sister,* there you're talking. Should have been a boy, that one. She plays in a team; wants to play rugby as well as soccer – great kid!'

At the same time, Dave – whose temperament and personality were anything but 'butch' and 'macho' – was interested in many things, all of which his father hated. 'I *mean,*' said Dave's father, indicating by his expression his feelings of repulsion, 'I mean, *poetry*! He reads poetry, makes the wretched stuff up himself – and painting pictures, that's another sissy thing. I blame all this Christianity, Bible-bashing stuff they've got him into at church. And that mate of his is no good to him either, looks like a stupid girl.' Dave had been told that his friend Sean, a boy from the same class at school, was banned from visiting Dave's house, and the same went for Dave visiting Sean's home.

In Chapter One, in relation to Erica, I introduced the term *conditional love*. Here I use the term *unconditional love*. Unconditional love in its most pure form persists no matter how 'bad' the object of that love. This does not mean that unconditional love *approves* of bad behaviour or sinfulness. God never stops loving us, but he does not overlook sin. However, in the behaviour of Dave's father we see an example of *conditional* love, a 'love' that seemed to say, 'I only love you when you are this kind or that kind of person, interested in *these* things, and fitting in with *my* concept of what you should be. I need you to become someone who will increase *my* prestige, causing *me* to be more admired and accepted.' Some parents who think like this are desperate for their children to shine in some spectacular way, such as gaining a first-class honours degree from a highly esteemed university, or requiring that their child should become a doctor, or if she is in the world of entertainment, a star – famous! This behaviour, in Christian terms, is a form of weakness, some would say sin, and in psychological terms it is often destructive. I am referring here not so much to the child's ambition, but to the parent's conditional love where that applies.

Dave's father would never have been physically cruel, but he was a very self-centred man. He would make fun of Dave, belittle him. He never condescended even to notice the boy's very lovely paintings, let alone praise or admire them. He was aware of his child's skill, of course, but did not want Dave to be 'encouraged' in it.

Dave's mother was kind and gentle, but expressed the view that she couldn't 'stand up' to her husband. However, she did manage to intervene to stop him from banning Dave from going to church. No one else in the family showed any interest in church-going. So here was a somewhat lonely child, suffering a great deal of stress. Dave was clearly a sensitive boy. By using the word 'sensitive' here I mean not that he was inherently weak, but that his emotions were strongly attached to beauty, colour and rhythm, and things spiritual. He was a boy experiencing conflict because one of his chief love and attachment figures, his father, was opposed to all that he, Dave, found fascinating and meaningful.

It may not be too strong to say that those people who opposed the idea of psychotherapy or counselling for Dave were unintentionally sinful – and there were some. In Dave's case it was the vicar of the church who persuaded Dave's mother to ask her GP about therapy. This is refreshing and encouraging – for sometimes we hear that clergy have dissuaded people from seeking such help – or even condemned it as something inherently dangerous and ungodly. Fortunately Dave's vicar was both godly and wise, for without the help Dave and his mother received at the clinic, the day might not have dawned, as thank God it did, when his mother and sister found their way to church. Whatever next? Or rather, *whoever* next – Dad!?

Some Christians take the view that nothing outside the individual person matters, and that as believers we should be only be interested in the individual soul, and in 'soul saving' (although in fact only God is able to save souls). This view rightly holds that the individual cannot excuse herself or himself for sinfulness on the grounds that things were against him or her (for example, that parents are to blame).

However, although there is truth in this view, it does not excuse any of us if we in our turn disregard evils that bear down on people and put them into situations whereby we ourselves would find it hard to resist temptation. Things 'outside' the person do matter – the sort of society we encourage matters, and it matters to God.

The Bible is brimming with accounts of whole societies and nations sinning (and being punished). We know of course that Israel herself, the 'Chosen People', sinned by turning to other gods. But God has always been interested, to put it into today's language, in putting right the so-called secular evils of society. In the fifth chapter of the Book of Amos (the prophet) the nation is blamed for such sins as skimping on measures in the market place and boosting prices, and cheating by the use of rigged scales, and selling the sweepings in with the wheat. In another book in the Bible, that of Hosea, the prophet, a terrible indictment is made against the whole nation because there is no truth or mercy, but there is lying and adultery, and there are drunken priests. The message seems to be: don't hide truth, don't reject mercy, don't pretend that the 'outside', the environment and the cultural background, does not matter – it does.

Children who are made 'scapegoats'

Emmanuel's problems

It will be as well to bear these thoughts in mind as I discuss Emmanuel, a third-generation black lad who was 13 when he was referred for help. At that time he was living in a residential establishment, the official name for what is often called a 'children's home'. The name of the establishment was Beechwood, and it was a voluntary organization (i.e. a charity) with a Christian ethic and partly motivated to bring children up, as they put it, 'within the Christian faith'.

Both Emmanuel's parents were alive and he had quite a clutch of siblings, all living at the parental home: four sisters and two brothers. So why was Emmanuel, alone, living in Beechwood? A simplistic answer to that question would be to reel off a list of some of the things he had done. For example, stealing. He had been in court on three occasions for this, larceny to be exact. Then there was setting fire to buildings, one appearance in court for this. Absconding (running away from home and sleeping rough) and truancy were also on the list. In addition to these escapades, he was a habitual liar.

So now we know why Emmanuel was in Beechwood – or *do* we? Do we even know what sort of lad he was? Was all this evil his own fault? Was there nobody else who needed to answer to God concerning Emmanuel's problems? We are writing here of a time, in Britain, when both the government and the opposition were fond of vying with each other for the 'best showing' on being 'tough on crime and tough on the causes of crime'. But what were the *causes* of crime in Emmanuel's case?

What do we know of Emmanuel's personality?

Staff members at Beechwood described him as sharp, intelligent, thrusting, sometimes manic, sometimes in the dumps, willing to 'get into scraps', but as having a good sense of humour. Some of them said that he could be quite fun to be with, but he also got moody and nasty when 'let down'. And he often got let down. Even in Beechwood he got let down time and time again, usually when members of his family failed to turn up to visit him after solemnly promising him they would.

This last observation, the broken promises, is a reflection of the way Emmanuel was treated by his family. For this lonely and rejected child, each time he stood peering out of the window in Beechwood, waiting, and finally giving up (and occasionally smashing something up), there was, as in Amos, *no truth or mercy*.

Recalling what I said in Chapter One about the development of the personality, about conditioning, about the attachment process, and the importance of love and care in the physical, mental and spiritual development of children, let's now look briefly at Emmanuel's history up to this point: his experience of childhood, the parenting he received and his sense of belonging.

For reasons we need not go into, Emmanuel's father disowned him at birth. His mother would sometimes protect him, but sometimes she would leave him behind, at the mercy of his father, when she 'took off' – that is, left the family home – with the rest of her children, sometimes for as long as ten days. More and more, Emmanuel was cold shouldered by the rest of the family. As the children grew they all tended to get into trouble by way of petty theft, vandalism and fighting, and generally making a nuisance of themselves in the neighbourhood and at school.

So how did the family as a whole deal with things when these youngsters got into trouble while Emmanuel was living with them, and on the few occasions when he went home 'on holiday' from Beechwood? All of them, father, mother and siblings, blamed Emmanuel. He became the scapegoat. If it were not for him, they lied to themselves, Dad would be happy, and nice. Mum would not keep leaving home. Gradually Emmanuel became an outcast. By the time he was six, the police had found him wandering the streets after midnight on three occasions. Eventually, for his own safety, he was put into local authority care by a juvenile court. Because of the hopeless lack of childcare facilities, Emmanuel experienced six placements (foster homes) before his tenth birthday. With each one he became more disturbed, more unhappy, more angry, and more 'difficult'. Scapegoating, once it starts, can go on and on.

Emmanuel began to experience the prejudice of other children, partly on account of his skin colour, and the exasperation of teachers who had not enough time to give him what he demanded – their *whole* attention. Everyone needs other people; we all need to feel accepted by someone. Possibly even St Paul himself did not realize how extensive in truth was his famous pronouncement: 'But the greatest of these is love' (1 Corinthians 13.13). So, like many excluded children, Emmanuel, who by now hated his name, found his friendships among other outcasts, the 'bad' boys and girls. At least among them he felt *wanted*, and he even felt important. They did not make fun of his name as one exhausted teacher had done – 'Emmanuel! God with us – God *help* us!'

And one of the things that made Emmanuel fly into a temper when he first arrived in Beechwood was the way some of the staff spoke of 'Father God'. 'Father' was a terrifying notion for Emmanuel. If God was like a father, he must be frightening and spiteful as well as rejecting. To pray to 'our Father' was at first impossible for him. But later, after months of real care and friendship, after months of unconditional love, together with counselling, Emmanuel began to respond in a positive way. And, yes, many prayers were said for him.

I cannot say how Emmanuel will turn out, what sort of an adult he will turn into, but we can see by his story so far that to a very great extent the things that have happened in his life, the way his own family rejected him – abandoned him in fact, will have helped to form whatever character emerges. He may become more aggressive and antisocial, he may become a depressive, or he could even turn against all that his family stood for and become absolutely honest – 'straight' (I've known that to happen). He could develop into an anxiety-ridden saint. One thing is certain, though, that until he changes and lives the life of a law-abiding person, if he ever does, events and 'things' outside him, his environment, will carry much of the blame for his delinquency – what's outside *does* matter. And on the 'outside', at the present time, are people who are sharing with Emmanuel the love they have for Christ. That name of his may turn out to be very meaningful after all.

Mixed-up adolescents and over-strict parents

Trixy's problems

Trixy was 14 when she first appeared at the psycho-therapy practice. Her parents and others described her as a 'thoroughly bad girl'. Like many thoroughly bad girls, she was a thoroughly pretty girl too.

How did this badness show itself? It showed itself in her running away from home, sometimes 'going missing' for the best part of a week and, as often as not, turning out to have been 'sheltered' by what might be called 'travelling folk' or men who operated the rides at travelling funfairs. This meant it also showed itself in her truanting from school. Then there was the glue-sniffing – she had sores all round her mouth and nostril area – and the smoking, not just ordinary cigarettes but 'weed', 'grass', 'pot' – marijuana.

How sad, what a criminal shame, a young girl, still a child really, and look at her. If only. If only Trixy had experienced a Christian upbringing and Christian influence, you might think. If only. But Trixy, I must now add, was the daughter of the minister of a local free church and, furthermore, she had 'given her life to Jesus Christ at the age of six'! But, in the solemn words of her father, 'By the age of ten she had *failed* to lead a life reflecting Christ'.

Trixy's mother, who had been a missionary, explained how her daughter had deteriorated. She had become ever more 'wilful'. First it was 'little things, like watching television programmes in other people's houses when she knows we don't approve of television at all, or allow it in our house'. Trixy's mother went on pouring out the negatives. Trixy 'could not be trusted'. She was described as 'a chronic liar'. For instance, there was the occasion where Trixy had said – with a perfectly straight face – that she was going to a meeting at church, when in fact it turned out that she had been to play with some 'heathen children' (albeit respectable ones!) whose parents allowed them to make pumpkin faces at Halloween. 'And I don't like to say this,' said Trixy's mother lowering her voice, 'but she *does* things to herself, you know, down there.' Masturbation, presumably.

For someone who had 'given' her life to Jesus at the age of six Trixy had, in the eyes of her parents, drifted off at a rate of knots as she grew older, so that at 12 she had not only used make-up outside, but gone to church with it on too. And then, of course, she had 'lied about it'. At 13 Trixy had declared that she hated church, hated her home, hated her parents, and had refused to say her prayers out loud when, each evening, the family gathered to pray as a family. Soon after this the running away started, and the escapades with 'men and boys – some of them real tramps!'

Most of you will have gathered enough from this account to be able to draw some conclusions as to whether or not Trixy's parents had erred. From Trixy's point of view, it would seem that being a Christian in a Christian family had

meant receiving the most burdensome and restricted childhood. Gradually, whatever pleasure or joy she experienced as
a little girl or a teenager had turned sour, so that she finally
gave in to some very real evils. There was no doubt that by the
age of 14 she seemed to be heading for a life of deep unhappiness. Soon she could be on hard drugs, and possibly suffering
from a serious sexually transmitted disease too.

So were her parents at fault? Had they driven their child in
the direction of drugs, promiscuity, and general bad behaviour? Such an idea shocked them and caused them to feel
angry and indignant, and they still could not believe that they
were in any way to blame. 'We live our lives, at least we try to,
according to biblical authority,' declared Trixy's father. He
protested that all they did, all the plans they made, were taken
each morning and each evening to the Lord in prayer.

To many of you, Trixy's parents will seem very narrow-
minded; to others, they may appear to be people who were,
indeed, living according to the Scriptures. When criticized for
this austere way of living, Trixy's father would readily quote
the Scriptures. He was fond of one passage from the epistle to
the Romans: 'Do not conform any longer to the pattern of this
world' (Romans 12.2). Likewise, his wife would defend their
decision not to have television in their home by quoting: 'Let
us purify ourselves from everything that contaminates body
and spirit' (2 Corinthians 7.1). In any case, they would point
out, what is the definition of 'austere'? Of course, it was
perfectly true that compared to many people in the world,
Trixy's parents lived in luxury, television or no television.
'Even running tap water', said Trixy's father, 'is a luxury to
some people in the world.'

The difficulty here is that so much of what Trixy's parents
were doing, the way they lived, and the way they made prayer
central to their lives, seemed on the face of it to be right, to be
pleasing to God. I would not criticize them for those aspects
as such. Perhaps, however, something was missing from this
family, not knowledge, or even love, or the Bible, but perhaps
– *wisdom*? Wisdom is not the same as knowledge. Wisdom

relates to the speed at which things should change, as well as direction; it can be concerned with *timing*. Jesus himself avoided his own arrest taking place at the wrong time. The question often arises, should parents pursue a way of life that would appear to be in some way painful, if not actually harmful, to their children, and yet seems to be a lifestyle (or even a mission) that enables them to do God's will? No doubt the answer will sometimes be 'yes', but parents must be very careful and very prayerful about what they see as a 'calling'. All of us must carefully examine our motives and seek pastoral guidance before taking up work that, for example, would separate parents and children during the important childhood and growing-up stages. And of course if parents do decide to stay with and nurture their offspring throughout childhood, and undertake no other 'jobs' outside the home, no one has the right to criticize them.

Sadly, it is all too easy for 'over-zealous' Christians to lose Jesus and find the Pharisees instead. It is so easy for ritual or form to take the place of the heart, so that instead of feeling the presence of the Spirit in the midst of the family, growing children feel the cramping, restrictive influence of dogma, or the mistaken interpretation of some dogmatic point. Did Trixy grow up with an image of God as reflected in his Son Jesus? Jesus who said he was her Shepherd, her Saviour, a light in her life to guide her? Was the Jesus she learnt about through her parents' way of life the same one who promised a comforter, and who said that if she had seen him she had seen her heavenly Father? Did Trixy know the Jesus of the Bible, or another Jesus who was only interested in how many times she knelt and prayed out loud, a Jesus who abandoned and condemned her because she watched television and put on make-up, as so many other children and teenagers do – including the ones who grow up to become adult believers? Which Jesus did Trixy know?

In case you are wondering just how far some 'enthusiasts for the word of the Lord' will go, here are examples of narrow-mindedness, and perhaps ignorance, when two such enthusiasts felt they were 'guided by the Spirit'. The first example concerns the author.

These days we are familiar with different English translations of the Bible. Most of the quotations in this book, for example, are taken from the New International Version (NIV), but one or two quote the Good News Bible (GNB). As a young man I entered the house of a 'keen Christian', an elderly lay preacher, who used only the King James Version, and upon showing him my 'modern translation' I was immediately ordered out of his house 'with that work of the devil'.

The second example concerns Anne Townsend, a very honest, self-searching Christian. Anne felt called to serve in the mission field, in Thailand. She even took her two-year-old daughter, Janet, with her and was already pregnant with her second child. Little Janet burned herself severely by sitting in some boiling jam, which was at floor level. Anne had to treat her daughter's terrible scalded areas, and of course she had to use lots of sheets and nappies. She writes:

> The last straw came when an over-zealous male missionary sought me out. 'I gather you're responsible for all the sheets on the washing line?' I nodded happily, assuming he would say how clean they were and what a good mother I was being. He grunted disapprovingly, 'You had them out on the Sabbath, yesterday. The Bible commands that we do not work on Sundays – you know that as well as I do. It's a terrible witness to all the villagers living around'. (Townsend, 1990, p. 50)

Can you find anything more pharisaic! It calls to mind the healings that Jesus did on the Sabbath, and the criticism he received. It also calls to mind Jesus' words to the Pharisees: 'The Sabbath was made for man, not man for the Sabbath' (Mark 2.27). That male missionary could not possibly have been reflecting the grace of his Master, and in many respects neither were Trixy's parents. 'The price of wisdom is beyond rubies' (Job 28.18).

So where did Trixy's parents go wrong? Did they in fact go wrong? I shall leave these questions for you to ponder.

Problems in integrating 'second families'

The Kingston family's problems

In this case we are concerned with 'parts' of two previously established families, which came together to form one new family group. This is a difficult situation, but is frequently seen today with the increase of second marriages following bereavement or divorce. The 'new family' comprised Ron Kingston and his wife Margery, and four children. Muriel, 12, and Jane, 10, were Margery's children by her first marriage. Ken, aged 11, and Susan, aged 9, were Ron's children from his first marriage. When I first met them, the Kingstons had been married for just over a year and things were going badly wrong in the new family.

Ten-year-old Jane had reached the stage of refusing even to speak to her new stepfather, while he had reached the stage of shouting at her – and even on occasions banning her from being in the same room as him. Muriel, Jane's sister, just about tolerated Ron, but became extremely jealous if her own mother expressed affection for either of Ron's children.

On the other hand, Ken and Susan seemed more than happy to accept Margery as their stepmother, and they needed all the mothering they could get. Their neediness, though, tended to cause problems between the two sets of children. To make matters worse, Jane linked 11-year-old Ken in her mind with his father (two alien males as far as she was concerned) and managed at times to set everyone else, or at least all the children, against Ken. Since he reacted by kicking her and pulling her hair, it meant that the two children carried on internecine warfare, especially on the way to church.

As for Ron and Margery, who had fallen in love when they met at a Christian holiday centre in Norfolk, they were both very unhappy and were 'wounding' each

other hourly with accusations and angry remonstrances.
They were, by turns, either in each other's arms, or
slamming doors behind them as each left the house not
to be seen or heard of for many hours.

Clearly, a very complex situation existed here, and so far I have
not even mentioned the relatives on each side! It is a fact that in
Britain and the United States, as well as in many other countries,
more and more family groups are comprised of parts of
previous families which have come together under second, or
even third, marriages or 'partnerships'. Although very many of
these 'new families' start by the couple falling deeply in love,
many end in a turmoil of accusation, disappointment and
anguish. Why does this happen? And before somebody says it
is because they have not committed the marriages to the Lord,
I have to say that even when both parents have been committed
Christians and have nurtured this new marital relationship,
many of these arrangements break down. Others, thank God,
move on from blessing to blessing.

    Although being aware that in all cases of human spite and
human destructiveness we are dealing ultimately with human sin,
we must nevertheless take note of the factors that bring unbear-
able stress into our lives, especially when that stress is itself the
result of human wilfulness, or in some cases 'social blindness'. If,
for example, we ignore the likelihood of the added stress that
comes from joining parts of established families, then we are
shutting our eyes when we ought to be taking stock, and trying
to foresee the problems and praying for insight.

    For this reason, I shall use some space in this section to look
at what we may call the 'chemistry' of a family, and the way
in which this chemistry is altered, or should alter, when a new
family is formed from parts of two or more families. As this
aspect forms a very extensive study within the areas of group
psychology and family dynamics, I shall be able only to touch
upon it here.

    By 'chemistry' we mean the dynamic of the family, the way
it functions; and this depends on many elements and other

variables such as the type of child discipline used, the degree of democratic interaction, the distribution of power within the family, the expression of affection (or lack of it), and the routines of daily life. Even such family idiosyncrasies as the Saturday morning 'lie-in' can become issues when the other half of the new family jumps out of bed at 6.00 a.m. regardless. The variations in living patterns are great, and include family routines such as who puts the children to bed, and whether or not they have a bedtime story. It includes mealtimes and how meals are taken – do we sit around a table, or stroll around the room eating 'on the hoof' and using our mobile phones at the same time? It deals with the minutiae of family life. The chemistry of a family is made up of hundreds of such elements, but they are not *all* minutiae. Even the emotional closeness of family members, and the quality of child–child and parent–child attachment, becomes part of the chemistry, part of the dynamic of the family.

The most important aspect to remember is that children growing up in a nuclear family are affected in many ways by the patterns set within that family. Some children come to value certain patterns or elements as experienced within their *first* family, sometimes called 'the family of origin'. True, some family experiences have the opposite effect. But, as an example of a disturbance very frequently met, I will mention the common negative reaction of children, especially adolescent children, at the prospect of their natural parents (Mum or Dad) remarrying and bringing another adult into the home – or even having to lose the 'home' and start in a new one. The frequent reaction is opposition to the idea, and turning the proposed stepparent into the enemy.

Sometimes a sibling group has developed its own pecking order in the original home. This is so particularly where parental control or influence has been weak or misguided. In certain situations this 'sibling dynamic', or 'sibling chemistry', can bring great difficulties when it comes to establishing a new family group. I have seen this when a sibling group of three or four children has been placed for adoption or has been fostered.

These days, even governments are pressing adoption organizations to place 'older children', and where possible to keep siblings together. This is a good idealistic aim, so long as everyone remains aware of the 'chemistry problems'.

A typical adopted sibling group is one I met that, prior to placement for adoption, had been members of a dysfunctional natural family where the children 'looked after themselves, and maintained discipline'. The second from eldest child had become the boss-bully. She kept some kind of order by a ruthless regime, which was a positive function up to a point because, being only 13 herself and having had a very unsatisfactory upbringing in a family where both parents were alcoholics, she could keep order by no other means. The two children below her in age viewed her methods as normal and regarded her as the family boss and organizer, while the one above was hardly ever there and lived a clandestine existence elsewhere.

Placing these children together within a new family led to enormous problems. This sibling group carried on with the pattern they had known and grown accustomed to. The younger ones listened only to 'big sister', who resented anyone else telling them what to do. Of course, it was right to want to give these children something else – a better family experience – but ignoring the family chemistry led to the placement 'breaking down', and all the children had to be removed, with consequent difficulties.

So how did the chemistry of the two families in the Kingston case affect the marriage and the uniting of the two sibling groups? We have already seen how the members from the two families were responding to each other. In order to help them, though, it was essential to know what demands were being made on individuals to accept (i.e. 'fit in with') family patterns that were alien or uncomfortable for them, and what behaviour patterns, beliefs and memories that had become special, even sacred, to them they were now being asked to give up. Such questions as the following seemed relevant. Had the parents come to terms with the 'loss' of their previous partners? What were the children's feelings concerning the 'loss' of one of their parents and the arrival of a stepparent? What were the patterns of living in the previous (natural) families? It turned out that some of the new and alien patterns were resented, and that there were unresolved 'feelings' in the family, especially in the case of the new Mrs Kingston with regard to her previous partner.

Ron said he was a Christian, and he certainly had a set of 'beliefs'. This set of beliefs included many activities that were mainly 'do's' and 'don't's'. He presented himself as being very moral – 'upright' was his word. However, 'Morality can be a cold and unyielding monster' (Todorov, 2000, p. 112).

Muriel and Jane, Margery's children, were young Christians in two senses. They were, after all, still children, but they were 'young', indeed 'babes', so far as their faith and Christian worship were concerned. Ron failed to appreciate that, and felt he had to 'set a Christian example of living' to these children. Presented with gentleness, patience and sensitivity, Ron's 'family prayers' and Bible readings each morning and evening might have been accepted by Muriel and Jane, but combined with timed homework that carried punishment for failure, as well as an 'everything in its place' household strictness, plus a very early bedtime with 'no talking after lights out', and three-times-a-day Sunday worship, none of Ron's 'regime' was accepted by the two girls.

Ron also 'believed in sport' and physical fitness, and these beliefs kept him away from his home quite a lot. He insisted on being on both his football team and cricket team committees, and of course playing these team games whenever called upon. Being a 'good Christian' and a keen churchgoer, he was also on three church committees. He was described by some people as a workaholic and it is easy to see why many of his family 'rules' had to be obeyed in his absence. He often arrived home tired and became angry when he found the rules being broken. Imagine the shock that this new family life had on Muriel and Jane.

Both these girls, and for that matter Margery, their mother, were expected by Ron to change in many ways. But it became clear that *Ron* also needed to change. In fact, the word 'change' must be seen as representing an important aspect of healing for the Kingston family. They really couldn't survive as a family group without change taking place.

Before taking a closer look at Margery's special need to change – that is, to change some of her personal, idiosyncratic ways – it will be helpful if I briefly describe one form of therapy made available to the Kingston family and that helped them all to change. The family *chemistry* had changed, not simply this or that individual. In other words, the dynamic of the family had changed.

The special form of therapy offered to the Kingston family is called *family therapy*. It is a form of group therapy in that the family is seen and treated together during the sessions. This does not mean that individual members of the family need to forgo individual or 'one-to-one' therapy, but it does mean that the family meet together with a trained family therapist. It is then interesting and helpful to watch the different slants emerging when a family, as a group, takes an active part in its own treatment. The interaction that takes place in the family group during this form of therapy is often very revealing, and it highlights factors that can be missed in other forms of talk therapy. The dynamic of the group emerges as the members each 'have their say' (or pull back and say nothing!) under the very light supervision of the therapist. It is often an uncomfortable form of treatment, especially for those at the top of the pecking order, because – when there is a skilful therapist to supervise – patterns of behaviour, and even motives, that were previously hidden begin to show up in a way that is different to that which occurs in individual therapy.

Something far-reaching developed during the family therapy concerning Margery Kingston – something that was already known to Muriel and Jane as their 'secret' about Mum. Certainly Ron had not caught on to it. It emerged that Margery was secretly bingeing. She was secretly stuffing herself with vast amounts of food, followed by several pints of water, and then making herself vomit by sticking her fingers down her throat. She had become bulimic.

I shall return later return to Margery, who clearly needed individual as well as family therapy. The family therapy, however, was helpful in revealing in a special way the fears held by the children. It enabled them to bring these out and talk about them. For example, Muriel's and Jane's fears and jealousies about the other children 'taking over' their mother were discussed. Having the 'other children' there actually helped. And Ron, although he kicked against it at first and became quite angry, eventually started to see himself as both unusual and draconian in his father role, and not very often being a true reflection of the Jesus he preached.

This unhappy family was not without prayer, and it was not without knowledge of the Bible. It was a family that was sharing lots of feelings but, as Ron admitted later, it seemed to be 'a family that was going nowhere except towards a break-up'. I'm glad to say that he was wrong.

Neither this case, nor the book as a whole, is meant to demonstrate 'psychotherapy to the rescue'. The Kingston case, despite all the aggravation and anger, is about a listening heavenly Father. God heard the anguished prayers of Margery. Her prayers involved the family situation and the bulimia, but both she and God knew something more.

Margery's first husband had been tragically killed in a traffic accident. The depression following that bereavement, and her feelings concerning the loss, had not really been resolved or, in everyday language, 'sorted out'. Margery had been left with a strange smouldering anger – something that is frequently encountered in psychotherapy. The anger, and this may come as a surprise, was directed towards her first husband. People may trivialize her feelings by saying that she 'couldn't forgive' him for dying. But it goes deeper than that and involves unnecessary 'guilt feelings'. In Margery's case, this was not guilt springing from some ordinary or extraordinary act of wickedness. Her mind, or her brain (or both, depending on one's belief system), had been affected by a devastating experience.

God has given us palliative medicines and also spiritual-counselling methods. He heard the prayers of Margery, Ron and the children. The family was led towards the sort of help I have described above – as many families have been led – and in Margery's case she was led forward into what some people call in-depth psychotherapy. Some people were surprised at the direction taken by God in the healing of this family – a family that later drew others into the joyous healing experiences of faith: 'In my distress I cried unto the Lord, and he heard me' (Psalm 120.1, AV).

Difficulties in being able to forgive a former partner

Samantha's presenting problems

Samantha described herself as a 'new Christian'. She also said she was very happily married. She had not been married long to Ben, and he had been a believer longer than she had. She described Ben as being 'full of life, love and logic', an interesting combination! Samantha had been previously married and her first husband was, as in the case of Margery Kingston, central to her problem.

'The fact is,' she said, during her first therapy session, 'that I am full of bitterness and anger towards Jerry, my first husband.' She then poured out much of her bitterness in angry statements, and it did seem to me that she had a case against Jerry. 'But', said Samantha, reaching for the tissues, 'since I've become a Christian I've forgiven him. But I'm still full of hatred, and thoughts about how I can fix him, or how he should be punished. This must mean that I'm not a Christian or . . . perhaps I haven't really got the Holy Spirit . . . or something.' Now she was weeping. After a minute or so she went on, 'This does affect my present marriage because it makes me irritable, and short-tempered with the children.'

Samantha had two children by her first marriage, six-year-old Jessica and four-year-old Erica. Jerry, their dad, had a legal right to access concerning the children, which meant that once a fortnight he had them with him for the weekend, plus he had them to stay with him for longer periods during the school holidays. During these access periods, Jerry, according to Samantha, used to lavish material wealth on the children. He was quite well off but kept Samantha short of money for the children's keep, telling her that as she now had a new husband and a job she didn't need financial help from him; and, what was more, he was hard up himself because of all his debts. Samantha burned with anger over this, because she and Ben – for all Ben's 'logic' – earned little by comparison, and were struggling financially.

What made Samantha want to put a bomb under Jerry, however, was that she knew, she insisted, that he 'stashed millions of pounds away in offshore banks' so that the authorities could never properly access his 'enormous' income. Her anger, and her desire to 'see him in hell', was stoked further when she learnt that he undermined the children's faith by ridiculing religion, Sunday school and the church at every opportunity.

So, despite Samantha's statement about being very happy in her new marriage to Ben, she clearly had moments of feeling very unhappy. She said she could not sleep at night and felt tired all day. She also suffered with pruritis (severe itching) 'all over my body – driving me mad'. Other somatic expressions of tension (see Jonathan's case in Chapter Three) developed as a result of her psychological and spiritual stress. She suffered at times from urticaria too, a kind of nettle rash characterized by weals and the appearance of redness over areas of her body.

Before going further and considering the broad subject area of forgiveness, revenge, anger and 'forgetting' (i.e. forgetting about harm done to oneself), we have to remind ourselves that the account given above concerning Samantha, Jerry and the children, albeit brief, is drenched in examples of 'sinfulness'. As I said at the start of this book, the fact of our considering these problems in the light of psychology and medicine in no way detracts from this underlying problem of humankind. And even if we exclude some of the people in the story from blame, we are still dealing overall with sin and evil – problems that affect *all of us*. Every one of us stands in need of grace, by which I mean the love of God bestowed upon us freely, undeservedly, completely and forgivingly. When Philip Yancey attempted to define 'grace' he finished up saying that it included these statements:

> There is nothing we can do to make God love us more,
> There is nothing we can do to make God love us less.
>   (Yancey, 1997)

Consider, however, what was happening in Samantha's case. There she was, allegedly being insulted, cheated on, in fear of being abandoned by the Holy Spirit, and wanting to see Jerry punished. But in fact all her anger and bitterness was punishing – who? Yes, Samantha herself. This goes on all over the world, angry and bitter people punishing and harming nobody but themselves. (Although, of course, some of them may be harming their children or other people they love as well.) 'Why', I often ask, 'let this person who has already hurt and cheated on you, do you further damage now at your own hand?'

Quite apart from the spiritual aspects of bitterness, brooding, holding a grudge and having feelings of revenge, there is clear medical and scientific research that shows that actual harmful changes take place in the body as a result of the sort of tension these feelings generate. I have no intention of turning this book into a medical textbook, but bear with me as I give a few examples. (If they want to, readers can further pursue the mind–body (body–mind) influence via library and internet exploration of the subject.)

If you have read the cases of both Bill and Jonathan (both in Chapter Three), you will be well aware of the rapid changes that take place within the nervous system, the endocrine system (hormones, etc.), and even the immune system, when an individual is subjected to stress. You will also be aware that some sorts of stress may be helpful and healthy while others, especially if persistent, may be harmful – and responsible for detrimental changes in the body.

Without becoming over-technical, here is a brief explanation of the way the immune system may be affected by chronic stress, the sort of continuing anger, bitterness and revenge stress that I am speaking of here. Most people will know that our bodies are protected all the time, every minute, by special cells that circulate in the blood and lymph systems. When we are invaded ('attacked') by bacteria or viruses, or affected by some of their poisons, these cells, which vary a lot as to their separate 'duties' or functions, come swarming out into the blood and the other systems and deal with these invaders and poisons.

Scientists have measured what happens in chronic stress. They have discovered that:

- Not as many of these defensive cells are produced in chronically stressed people, and
- The average number circulating is below the level circulating in non-chronically stressed individuals.

There is also a suspicion, with further research still ongoing concerning this, that the fighting power ('cytotoxicity') of these cells is reduced by chronic damaging stress. All this means that the immune system becomes downgraded and that people carrying chronic, damaging stress may become more vulnerable to illness.

Apart from the immune system, however, many other changes take place in stress so that the chemistry of the body changes. Short-term changes are acceptable so long as we are not talking about extreme, e.g. shock, changes. In fact, they signal that the body is functioning properly, and I have already referred to the 'fight or flight' mechanism that ensures that when a person is faced with something frightening or threatening, the body reacts automatically in a way that speeds up the heart rate. This prepares the person to fight, or run like the wind. We needed this when tigers prowled around. But if we were to arrange our lives and environments so that our heart rate was speeded up all or most of the time, we should soon suffer from heart failure. Unfortunately damaging chronic stress does something rather similar to us.

It would be possible to produce a lot more evidence to show that psychological stress, such as chronic anger or envy or a continuous burning wish to see one's enemy hurt, damages the body and downgrades the health. I am of course generalizing, and people react in different ways to different experiences. But before discussing forgiveness, something central to Samantha's problem, it seems important to make it clear that, apart from anything else, being able to lose bitter feelings will bring blessings in physical terms as well as spiritual ones. Samantha's pruritis and urticaria appeared to be connected to the stress she put upon herself. As you read this, you may feel quite angry with Jerry. However, Samantha's own reactions were damaging only herself. Her problem, though, was really quite complex. Intellectually she had 'forgiven' Jerry, but emotionally she continued to experience the same feelings she had before she had forgiven him.

It is important for readers to appreciate that we are dealing here with a subject that, were I to examine and enlarge on all its aspects, could take up several chapters. To begin with, there is the ongoing argument concerning who is in the position to forgive and who may be forgiven. Also, there is the debate concerning exactly what is meant by 'forgiveness' or 'forgiven'. Some writers equate forgiveness with reconciliation, but reconciliation is only possible when two (or more) parties want to come together, desire to explore and see where each may have been 'wrong', and so forth. If one party has no intention of reconciliation and continues to persecute or otherwise pursue a course aimed at hurting or harming the other, or simply not bothering how the other is affected ('well, tough luck, keep out of my way'), does it become even ethical to say, 'Never mind, I forgive you, carry on as you are doing'? Should not forgiveness be something granted by one person to another when there has been an expression of regret about previous behaviour and a request (expressed or implied) for forgiveness? One thing seems certain – forgiving does not mean approving of behaviour that has been hurtful or, in more general terms, sinful.

Yet we are asked to forgive. One writer, Russ Parker, says, 'Jesus expected his disciples to be forgivers. What is also important is that he did not regard this as an option but a commitment' (Parker, 1993). But we still need to know what is meant by the word 'forgive'. Remember, our Bible is a translation. We are not reading it or understanding it in the original language. And even when we have translated it, the words we finish up with may change their meaning over time. Yet again, I promise – as I did when talking about the biological effects of stress – that I shall not turn this section into a deep theological thesis or an essay on the meaning of certain Greek or Latin words. However, I think it will be useful to look at this a bit more.

The 'forgiveness' message that comes over from a study of the different biblical (Greek) words appears to be about 'debts cancelled', or 'debts remitted'. So far as human forgiveness is concerned, it is about letting people off punishment that is deserved or debts that are due; it is about *cancelling* debts, not only money debts, but what we may call 'getting even debts'. The message is not about ignoring sin or even forgetting it. The forgiveness message is about not wanting to 'pay some-one back', and not wanting to 'get my own back'. Often, in the Authorised Version (King James' Version) of the Bible the word 'remission' is used concerning God's forgiving of human sin. In a modern English dictionary the verb 'to remit' has the definition 'to cancel or refrain from exacting or inflicting (a debt or punishment etc.)' (*Concise Dictionary*, W. H. Smith, 1991).

Of course, God's forgiveness is absolute, and in his forgive-ness, through Christ, our sins are forgiven. Talking of humans forgiving one another, W. E. Vine (1985) points out that in the case of human forgiveness certain conditions are involved, and he refers to Luke 17.3f: 'If your brother sins, rebuke him, and if he *repents*, forgive him' (my italics), and also to Matthew 18.15–17. This passage has the same message as that quoted from Luke, but our English version avoids the harsh word 'rebuke', and says 'go and show him his fault'. But even in this Matthew version, 'if he refuses to listen to the church', he is not to be seen as acceptable.

What Samantha needed to do, as a Christian, as a sensible person, as someone wishing to act in the best interests of her health and the well-being of her family, was to drop the desire to exact punishment on Jerry, or the wish to see him punished and brought low. She needed to be able to 'remit', to cancel in so far as a human being can, the debt, the punishment, and the desire for punishment and revenge. Samantha needed to be able to change her attitude and feelings so that her theme might become, 'I would have liked Jerry to have apologized and to have changed his behaviour, but I cannot force him to do so. I will now leave punishment or retribution to the One all wise, all-loving God. I will *let go* of anger; I will *let go* of hatred and feelings of revenge. I shall be free. I shall be calm and at peace in Christ and my heavenly Father.'

So many of us have been brought up in a culture of 'getting even'. We have been programmed to feel that somehow we are disgraced if we do not retaliate. But quite often there is very little a person can do to change things in the way they would wish. I have met people who were burning with anger towards someone who had died! 'Why did he do this to me?' And other people who were bitter at the way 'life' had treated them – and 'cheated' them. They had spent 50 years destroying their bodies and warping their minds.

This is not an endorsement that Christians should become 'doormats' and never show disapproval or anger. But it is a recommendation to search for other insights and other attitudes. It is a plea that we listen to God, to the 'still small voice', and to let him release us from our prisons. We are often prisoners of events, of memories, of 'principles', and angry outcomes. Russ Parker, again, writes:

> . . . although we cannot be responsible for the things that have happened to us, we must be responsible for the way we have responded to those things. It is this step of accountability which is actually the threshold of healing because by the Grace of God we can be changed from being the prisoner of our past and choose a new response through the power of the Holy Spirit within us (Parker, 1993).

It was this experience of the deep difference between the intellectual act – in her case, 'I've forgiven him' – and the emotional *letting go* of self-destroying resentment that eventually brought so much healing to Samantha. 'Healing', it has been said, 'is not God doing something to us, but rather doing something with us.'

Samantha could not literally forget Jerry's behaviour. It was ongoing, in any case. Some counselling has left people with feelings of guilt because they could not forget incidents – be left with no memory of them. This is faulty counselling. Nobody, unless severely injured on the head or doped with drugs or suffering from a brain-deteriorating disease, can forget, simply as a result of forgiving. Sometimes, as a result of trauma, blocking-out of memory may occur, but this was not that kind of case. No, Samantha was able to respond and feel differently not because she forgot, but because she was enabled to *let go*. Although she came to it by prayer, thought and counselling, she realized later that she had fulfilled St Paul's advice: 'Do not take revenge, my friends, but leave room for God's wrath, for it is written: "It is mine to avenge; I will repay," says the Lord' (Romans 12.19).

Other physical conditions that affect our emotions

Sula's presenting problems

> Sula was 46, married, with two grown-up sons aged 20 and 22. When we first met she was a most unhappy woman who truly reflected her husband's description when he said, 'Sula's changed, I've lost her. She seems to be in some kind of deep pit, unable to get out.'
>
> For one thing, she could not stop crying. She was very depressed, so much so that she even spoke about there being no point in going on living. But how could a believer, 'a strong Christian' as her husband had called her, come to feel like this? What about those lovely, helpful, uplifting Bible verses she had been so fond of quoting, even if she did run them into one another: 'Do not let your hearts be troubled. Trust in God; trust also in me. Peace I leave with you; my peace I give you. I do not give to you as the world does. Do not let your hearts be troubled and do not be afraid' (John 14.1 and 14.27)? And what about the psalms she had quoted and learnt by heart? Such verses as 'God is our refuge and strength, an ever-present help in trouble' (Psalm 46.1) spring to mind. Sula was not angry with God, nor had she lost her faith. Neither she nor her family, nor her friends, could understand why she felt so sad – so without that special *peace*.

Some people, however, felt they knew why she was 'upset', but they still could not understand why Sula was so depressed. They felt she was depressed about her elder son, Ralph, who was at university. About six months before she came for therapy, Ralph had returned home for the Christmas vacation and had shocked his mother, and to some extent his father and brother too, by declining to attend the Christmas morning church service and declaring that he was no longer a Christian and had no intention of 'pretending' any more. For Sula – who had prayed daily for her son ever since she first knew she was pregnant, who had with intense belief told her child the Bible stories in his infancy, and had waved him off to university with the words 'God bless, Ralph. We'll be praying for you – I love you!' – it had obviously come as a great blow to hear he was now to turn his back on God. And because she was a 'strong' and rather sensitive believer, she began to worry about his ultimate salvation.

Sula, who had invested so much in what she called 'Bible truth', had turned other verses over in her mind, such as, 'God raised him from the dead on the third day . . . everyone who believes in him receives forgiveness' (Acts 10.40, 43). But Ralph did not believe in him, Ralph had rejected him! Then there was the verse, 'Therefore, there is now no condemnation for those who are in Christ Jesus' (Romans 8.1). But could Sula now tell herself that her son was '*in* Christ Jesus'?

Perhaps Sula forgot at that miserable time that God is sovereign and that ultimately he will rule and overrule: 'The sovereign LORD has filled me with his spirit' (Isaiah 61.1, GNB), and in Psalm 97: 'The LORD reigns, let the earth be glad; let the distant shores rejoice' (Psalm 97.1). Essentially she was setting aside the words 'the Lord reigns' and now found it hard to be comforted by them. In fact, I believe it is not 'by luck' that prayerful people like Sula have found their way to particular therapists. As a psychotherapist, I have always been alert to the possibility of misdiagnosis, which even good but busy GPs can occasionally make in the early stages of a physical condition. When I had seen Sula for the third time, I became uneasy about her diagnosis of 'depression' on its own. Yes, Sula was depressed, but she showed other symptoms such as feeling cold, feeling 'tingling' and numbness in her fingers, and she complained of a hearing loss. These and the other symptoms she spoke of are not usually part of the psychological condition we term 'depression'; and, what's more, Sula appeared to get no better as a result of psychotherapy alone. I asked her to see her GP again, who then did certain blood tests.

The result of these tests was that a new diagnosis was made – she was hypothyroid. What did that mean? Briefly, it meant that one of the many hormones (chemical substances) normally flowing in Sula's body, as in everyone else's, was not being produced in a sufficient quantity to regulate the function (metabolism) of the body. It meant that the hormone thyroxine, produced in the thyroid gland (found in the neck), was being underproduced. Another symptom of a hypothyroid condition is extreme fatigue, which Sula experienced. Given the right medical treatment, medicine in the form of synthesized thyroxine, Sula soon recovered her previous vitality and optimism.

I have deliberately in this book focused on problems that arise from the interaction between people and problems and that could relate to environmental and attitude factors. True, in some sections I have touched on physical causation – as I did when considering the case of Ron and Sally in Chapter Two. In that case, as well as the interactions and motivations of several people, there was also the extreme premenstrual stress (or syndrome), PMS, which is related to hormonal changes.

In this section, having looked at Sula's case and noted the fact that physical illness may affect the way people behave, I feel it might be useful to take the discussion further.

Some 'religious' people become rather worried when they learn that a person's behaviour may be directly affected by a bunch of hormones! In that case, they ask, where has 'free will' and self-determination gone? How can God ask us to do his will if our endocrine glands are going to make us depressed, angry or even suicidal when we have no 'reason' (or desire) for such feelings? Where does my soul come into it if I'm motivated by chemicals?

We need to reflect a little here. After all, when people drink too much alcohol their personality may be (temporarily) changed. They may act in outrageous, silly, dangerous, and even violent ways. We know that the alcohol has interfered with the normal working of the nervous system. We also know that to drink alcohol to excess, and in some circumstances to drink alcohol at all, is to go against God's wishes and his plan.

But when we think about drug-taking (and alcohol is a drug), and think about altering the function of the brain in this way, we do not feel that 'the soul' has been lost or destroyed or doesn't exist.

We have to accept that in our present human form we *are* 'flesh and blood'. But we believe that, in a manner that is still beyond what we call 'science', we are also a complex function of body–mind–soul, and that in our present state each of these aspects of the human has to function in the way God designed it to function in health, and within an environment that supports a healthy life. The three aspects of body–mind–soul are, for the time being, interrelated.

Because of this interrelationship, disease, dysfunction or poisoning of the body may affect the way we feel (in emotional terms) and, because of this, the way we behave. Organic dysfunction may cause what can often be mistaken as an exclusively psychological disorder. Take, for example, the very opposite of Sula's condition – *hyperthyroid*. Hers was *hypo*, i.e. insufficient. With a *hyper*thyroid condition, which means too much thyroxine is produced, the patient may present with 'manic' symptoms (being overactive, overexcited) and also develop concentration problems, memory impairment and what therapists call 'emotional lability' (feeling euphoric one moment and weepy the next).

To illustrate my point still further I can describe the way a person's emotional state may be affected by a similar under-functioning of a different gland, the pituitary. This small gland is situated at the base of the brain. If it is under-functioning (i.e. *hypo*pituitarism) the patient may present with severe depression, but s/he may *also* suffer from loss of appetite to the extent that the person loses weight and may even begin to look like the kind of body we see in the anorexia nervosa patient. There have been cases of misdiagnosis whereby the person has been 'treated' with antidepressive drugs and psychotherapy, and only been correctly diagnosed when the illness became more advanced. Worse still was the case of one young woman whose Christian friends criticized her for 'lack of faith' on account of her deep depression, when in fact she was suffering from a glandular dysfunction such as I've described above.

I have said enough to show that sometimes anxiety and depression, and even anger, may develop because of an organic dysfunction. From a Christian point of view, it is possible to see these symptoms as resulting from an 'evil', i.e. the evil of disease or of organic dysfunction, but not necessarily resulting from individual sin.

A word of caution, though. This book is intended to *help* anxious people (not worry them!), so please do not jump to the conclusion that you are suffering from a hypothyroid, hyperthyroid or any other glandular dysfunction just because you feel angry or a bit depressed, or you can't concentrate. The truth is that we all experience these feelings from time to time. Do not be afraid to seek the kind of help advocated in this book, but for most times, and for most passing ailments, if your doctor has seen you and assured you, then: 'Commit your way to the LORD; trust in him . . .' (Psalm 37.5).

Sula found that special peace again. She prays for Ralph, she commits him to God, and she leaves the matter 'in God's hands'.

Feeling condemned by God

Daniel's presenting problems

'I believe in God. I believe in Jesus Christ,' said Daniel at his first session, 'but I do not believe I'm forgiven; in fact, I believe I'm damned, I'm a sinner. Because of what I've done I can't be saved, I can't be forgiven.'

Daniel agreed that there were other times – 'fleeting moments' he called them – when he felt he *might* be forgiven and he *might* be able to 'make amends'. He used phrases like that – 'make amends', 'earning God's love', or 'earning God's forgiveness'. He was not sure whether his negative thoughts, those dismal 'no hope' thoughts, made him as anxious as he often became, or whether it was some kind of permanent depression or free-floating anxiety that made him keep having the dark thoughts about sin and his own *inevitable* ever-lasting condemnation.

'I can't get rid of these thoughts,' he would plead, 'the Bible says I'm condemned.' Then he would say, 'Those who have done good will rise and live, and those who have done evil will rise to be condemned – John 5, verse 29.' Another passage he was likely to quote was from Jesus' parable about the vine. He would remind people that: 'If anyone does not remain in me, he is like a branch that is thrown away and withers; such branches are picked up, and thrown into the fire and burned', which comes (out of context) from John 15.6.

It is possible, therefore, to describe Daniel's central present-ing problem as 'religious' or 'existential'. Even if it were eventually discovered that this religious slant were a symp-tom and that there were other factors producing the anxiety, I would still describe these negative religious thoughts as his 'presenting problem'. Daniel came for help because he could not deal adequately with these foreboding thoughts, with these 'truths' as he saw them. Notice that I said we can describe his anxiety as centring on religious or 'existential' matters. Readers may recall that I used the term 'existential' to describe some of Bill's problems (Chapter Three), when I explained that it referred to the beliefs and attitudes and anxieties that have to do with the meaning and purpose of life, of existence, of *being*. Daniel clearly believed that with human beings, existence involved an 'after death' state. He also *believed* that God is interested in *measuring out* what each of us deserves. I have emphasized the word 'believed' here because the beliefs we hold affect our attitudes, and attitudes are related to emotions.

It was possible to see in Daniel's condition elements that are quite common to many people. I have said above that some beliefs and attitudes are strongly related to emotions. This is not always obvious, nor is it fully recognized that some emotional attachments make it difficult for people to change their beliefs and behaviour. For example, Daniel would have found it extremely difficult to break with the beliefs of his parents because he was so emotionally attached to them, and they had impressed upon him from early childhood the 'wrongness', indeed the *wickedness,* of displeasing God, and the equal 'wrongness' of disloyalty to parents.

According to Daniel, many, many things he did as a child displeased God. As far as he was concerned, things he had said, things he had done to other children ('typical' boyish behaviour really – things like not giving his last sweet away, and tugging at little girls' plaits), and even many things he had thought about – especially during adolescence – were anathema to God. God, for Daniel, was forever on watch, on the look out; God was a mighty power who kept an accurate account of deeds done, and of deeds left undone, but he wasn't much else.

All this 'knowledge' about God left an impression on Daniel's mind as he grew up. He received such 'knowledge' (given with the finest of loving intentions) at two and a half years old, at six years old, at 15 years old, at . . . ? But wait. His mother died when he was 16. This was devastating for Daniel. This was the mother whom Daniel adored. He swore to himself he'd keep faith with his mother for the rest of his life. He would remain loyal in all his ways – and in his beliefs.

I am not saying that this upbringing itself was directly responsible for Daniel's existential problems. As a matter of fact he had a brother who experienced the same family upbringing and the same picture of God, and of course the same loss of a loving mother. But Bob, his brother, was not Daniel. What he 'did' with his 'experience' was different. Daniel did not have Bob's personality and vice versa. Because he was Daniel and not Bob, he was more likely, when anxieties or guilt feelings approached, to link these to earlier life experiences and to be controlled by fixed attitudes: to attitudes and loyalty feelings that he did not always recognize were controlling him.

Furthermore, Daniel had a belief in a vicious God – his mother's God? She was a kind person, so what had gone wrong? It would now be difficult to trace where the image of God as 'all revenge and punishment' had come from. No doubt many teachers, preachers and others had emphasized what they saw as aspects of God, but sadly they had failed to give Daniel the true image as revealed in the Bible.

There were two avenues of discovery that helped Daniel to overcome his crippling thoughts. One was to learn more about his own self, his own reactions, his own deeply held convictions and why he could not easily let go of these. The other, the more important as it turned out, was to learn more about what the Bible says about God and to discover that Daniel's image of God belonged much more to the Pharisees and the Old Testament than to that painted by Jesus Christ, Son of God.

On his third or fourth session I offered Daniel a book to read. It was called *What's So Amazing about Grace?* (Yancey, 1997). It was the beginning of a new spiritual insight for him. Even that word 'grace', used so often, heard so much in church, suddenly revealed the most startling aspect of God, an aspect that would have been blazing out all the time in the story of Jesus Christ if only the teachers and preachers had switched on its light. Even from several of the parables that Daniel had heard over and over again ever since nursery school, there now emerged for him new teachings. He had previously thought that the parable of the lost son (often called the parable of the prodigal son) was there to teach people how to seek forgiveness. It was there, he thought, to let people know that the wretched lad who had left home and squandered all the hard-earned money his father had scraped together over the years would receive his just deserts by having to creep back and humbly beg for forgiveness.

Daniel was wrong about that story. Completely, utterly, hopelessly wrong. It turned out to be a story about a *father* whose heart ached every day he woke to count it one more day not knowing where his cherished son was. It turned out to be a story about a father who could not even stand still and await the arrival of his son on the doorstep. Instead this father *ran* towards his son: 'he ran to his son, threw his arms around him and kissed him' (Luke 15.20). It was, what's more, a story reflecting the love, compassion and forgiveness of God. That was the point of the parable.

Then there was the story of the lost coin. In spite of the verses that speak of the rejoicing of the angels of God, Daniel had focused only on the woman's search, and her sweeping out the whole house until she found the coin. For Daniel, this search represented the 'work' he must do to appease God. Daniel's old God was a God of appeasement. But the point of the story, he discovered, was about how valuable Daniel himself was in God's sight; it was about a compassionate and loving God who loves *individuals*. The one lost coin was valuable to the woman. One lost soul is infinitely valuable to God.

Another parable Daniel had wrongly interpreted until he read Yancey's book was the parable of the lost sheep. Actually, to human eyes, this was about a *ridiculous* shepherd who, as Yancey points out, goes and leaves 99 sheep exposed to danger and searches for just *one* that had wandered off – ridiculous indeed! No, it is not ridiculous. Daniel came to realize that he himself, the sheep that was lost, one individual, was *precious* to God. That was the point of the story!

So Daniel came to understand something about the grace of God. He had previously 'received' a message that God treated us as we deserve to be treated. He and his family, his parents, etc., were very fair-minded, honest people. They never cheated, and they always gave praise where it was deserved. But the truly astonishing lesson Daniel learnt was that God does not give us what we *deserve*. Philip Yancey has written, 'In the realm of grace the word deserve does not even apply' (Yancey, 1997). If God gave us what we deserved there really would be no hope, but God's grace has ensured that a price – a tremendous price – has been paid, and now we can be set free through his grace.

Daniel was particularly moved by a story told by Ernest Hemingway and repeated by Yancey. It concerns a Spanish father who decides to reconcile with his son who had run away to Madrid. The remorseful father has an advertisement inserted into the *El Liberal* newspaper, 'Paco meet me at Hotel Montana noon Tuesday. All is forgiven, Papa'. Paco is a common name in Spain, and when the father goes to the square he finds 800 young men named Paco waiting for their fathers – waiting for forgiveness!

Hemingway himself had experienced what Yancey calls *ungrace* for many years from his parents, themselves brought up as evangelical Christians. One message Hemingway's mother gave him was to the effect that a mother's life is like a bank. Every child, she said, is born with a seemingly inexhaustible bank account of care-giving. In the early years the child makes withdrawals but no deposits. And when the child grows up, it is her/his responsibility to replenish the supply by caring deeds towards the parents.

This is the bank-balance, economic attitude. It is concerned with earning one's place. Many religions carry that idea, and Daniel had been brought up affected by it. But the grace of our Lord Jesus Christ is not concerned with economics or account balancing. The price has been paid in and through Jesus Christ. Grace does not make economic sense, but it saves us! Grace, God's grace, is set totally apart from so much of what our secular culture teaches. We hear, 'There's no such thing as a free lunch', 'The early bird gets the worm', 'No pain, no gain', 'You get what you pay for', and 'Demand your rights' and so on (Yancey again). Certainly we should expect children to show loving care towards parents, but Hemingway himself felt rejected by *ungrace*.

Daniel even thought that the parable about the workers in the vineyard, which in economic, trade-union and boss–worker terms makes no sense at all, was told by Jesus to help his listeners to learn not to grumble about their lot in life. In that parable the men who worked for only half-an-hour got paid as much as those who had toiled in the sun all day – not fair! Quite so, it was not meant to be about 'fairness'. It was a totally new message, which said, 'My grace has nothing to do with earning power, it comes to you free.'

Partly because of his personality and basic temperament, partly on account of the loss of his mother, partly because of a wrong interpretation of the meaning of the 'anger of God', which made it sound like some kind of petty, ill-tempered, human spitefulness, and partly because of the many 'don't's' he experienced in his 'religious' life (almost 'don't rejoice – you have no right to feel happy') and many more such factors, Daniel was experiencing Christianity in somewhat the same way that the Pharisees experienced Judaism: being completely hemmed in by rules ('laws') of ritual and outward symbolism. But with his new understanding of his Saviour, Christ Jesus, Daniel realized for the first time the force and meaning of the words, 'For the law was given through Moses; grace and truth came through Jesus Christ' (John 1.17). Daniel now *believed* that he could be forgiven – and I believe that too. However, although he became a changed and happy man, he continued to believe that *without* the price paid by our Saviour, and unless we turn to him and away from sin, spiritual death is a reality. (I shall pick up on this point again in Chapter Five.)

This brings us to the end of the individual 'presenting problem' discussions. Although Chapter Five is very different, and deals in a broad way with human psychology and behaviour, I shall draw on the cases discussed in these last three chapters to illustrate my points.

(Note: Apart from individual readers gaining something from the book up to this point, the case discussions can be used for seminars and student group discussions, as well as in church house groups.)

Five

The main purpose of this book has been to show that modern physics requires the God principle.
Frank J. Tipler, in *The Physics of Immortality*

In this final chapter I shall review much of the material in the preceding chapters. However, I shall not do this case by case, but by looking at broad aspects. For example, most of the cases outlined have carried descriptions of how individuals related to one another. That is to say they were concerned with *interaction*, the way two or more people interacted. Therefore we will look more closely at this.

There are other aspects to be considered in this way. One area of study, although it needs breaking down a bit, could go under the general heading of *feelings*: the way the different clients or patients felt, and feelings they had at different times, is important, so we shall have a closer look at this too.

What do we believe? What do we imagine?

Straightaway we need to begin to chop up some of these words in order to better understand these questions. In so many of the cases discussed in this book, the element of *belief* enters and plays a vital part. But quite often the words 'belief' and 'believed' did not appear in our discussions. Moreover, because this book is written from a Christian point of view, as soon as I use the word 'belief', as I did above when I referred to an 'element of belief' entering in, the reader could be excused for thinking I was referring to Christian belief: that is to say, a belief in Jesus Christ and faith in him. Mostly, though, the people I discussed were suffering on account of what they believed or imagined about themselves and other people.

I wrote in Chapter Two about Anne. She had become agoraphobic and was unable to leave her house without experiencing panic attacks. She *believed*, wrongly, that she had a physical (organic) illness causing this. She also *believed* that God might be punishing her. Marilyn (Chapter Three) exhibited another form of 'belief'. She, you may remember, could not rid her mind of terrible thoughts, which kept coming back no matter how silly she felt them to be when she reflected on them. Yet, when the thoughts were there they made her frightened of herself. She loved her husband and her two young children but felt (believed? imagined?) that one day she might cut the throats of her infants while they slept. She trembled when she reported these obsessional thoughts to her therapist, and she said, about the throat cutting, 'Yet I know I wouldn't.' So what did she really *believe*?

Although we use the same word 'believe', we are clearly talking about different experiences and different thought processes when we say 'I believe in God' or 'I believe I'm being followed' or 'I have this horrible thought that haunts me – I believe I might cut my children's throats, but I know I wouldn't'. Sometimes we appear to be talking about hard physical facts, and the idea of believing comes into our thinking though we don't have to spell it out. We often say 'I know', such as 'I know that three plus three makes six', and of course we believe this to be true. Sometimes we may talk about things physical and all our 'facts' may be anything but true yet we can't stop believing them to be true. This is particularly relevant to hypochondriacs, and there are a great many of them. There are millions of perfectly healthy people who are convinced (at least, every two weeks they are convinced) that they have a life-threatening disease; they *believe* it. It does not seem to matter how many times they have been told on good professional medical authority that their heart is strong, healthy and superbly functioning, the slightest ping and they are off again – dying! There are also lots of people, especially males, who, upon reaching 48–50, are convinced that they are 'finished' (i.e. they believe they are), even though they are quite healthy and are good for an active

life for another 30 or even 40 years. Accepting then that we are
including many different concepts when we employ the word
'believe', and even when we simply imply 'belief', I want now
to consider the question: Do our beliefs affect us physically,
mentally and spiritually?

Consider this account: recently a medicine, a new drug, was
tested for marketing. One part of the test involved taking two
sets of people and giving set 'A' the real drug, while 'B' had only
a placebo, something just made of a white paste and having no
chemical (medical) properties. Of set 'A', those on the real drug,
36 per cent of the patients showed 'improvement', but of the
patients who had just the paste, the placebo, 56 per cent of these
patients showed 'improvement'. So the new drug was not put
on the market, as it could not be said to uphold the claim of the
manufacturers. But what had happened to the 'B' set of
patients? It seems that the 'improvement' came about as a result
of what they *believed*. These people accepted that they were
being helped; their minds and bodies did the rest. How strong
can the power of the mind be? How much effect can belief have
on the health, and even the life-span, of the body? (Many other
similar experiments and examples such as the one above could
be cited, but sadly lack of space precludes this.)

Sometimes – and we have already given illustrations of this
– belief may lead to anxiety, or even to depression. Belief,
however, may also lead to joy, exhilaration and to a healthier
body. In Chapter Four we presented and discussed the case of
Samantha, who you will recall was 'full of bitterness' (her own
words). She also believed that despite her other description of
herself as 'a new Christian', her bitterness and anger must mean
that she was not a Christian. So there she was, carrying a great
conflict around with her. And what was all this doing for her
body? She suffered from skin problems: urticaria and pruritis.

It is interesting to speculate: does it work the other way
round? Are people who feel no anxiety, and who never experience sickness to any degree, happy and contented people? This
is a difficult question to answer because there does not seem
to be a lot of research that has looked at 'happy people' and

measured their illness rates. In any case, in purely secular terms, what is a happy person? However, there is a good deal of research that appears to indicate that a mind (brain) free from stress, anxiety and depression is likely to influence the body in a way that tends to keep it healthy. Bear in mind that at present I am considering the 'secular' approach, although it is likely that many people in these research findings who did feel secure were in fact people who believed in some religion, even if not the Christian faith. Some of these secular studies have shown that the way people interpret and experience their lifestyle – in other words what they come to *believe* about themselves – affects their health. For instance, dissatisfaction with growing old is associated with an increased mortality rate. Increased mortality has been associated in some studies of the elderly with depression and lower self-esteem, and also with less social interaction and fewer friendships.

An interesting piece of research was carried out in the 1970s concerning Japanese people who had emigrated to the United States. It was known that, speaking generally, Japanese who lived in Japan had heart rates one-fifth of the level of Japanese living in the United States. However, two epidemiologists identified a group of Japanese immigrants in California whose heart rates and rates for diseases of the heart were the same as for those Japanese living in Japan. This healthier group had retained the cultural, religious, social and other Japanese living and thinking styles. Listed below are a number of beliefs that, it has been noted, have been held by 'exposed' and 'at risk' children who nevertheless survived – in that they did not, as many have done, succumb to pressures that would have driven them towards delinquency or self-harm. The list is my own, but it is derived from the research and the book by Mark Katz (1997). Remember, this was purely secular research:

- The belief that they are valued by certain other people.
- The belief that the world is, by and large, 'benevolent'.
- The belief that the world is meaningful.

- The belief that it is OK to express emotions.
- The belief that people are prepared to help you.

They also experienced:

- A sense of hope, and a sense they could also offer help to others.

My reason for looking at this secular research is to emphasize the fact that the way we live, and what we believe in, really does affect our health, and that although as Christians we believe that the highest fulfilment of these health-giving attitudes and lifestyles is to be found in union with God, as God intended, we can see that even on a more mundane level God's plan of spirit, mind and body working in harmony may be glimpsed.

Here are some biblical words. See how thousands of years ago God gave to human beings advice that we in the twenty-first century find confirmed as wise advice and good science:

> A cheerful heart is good medicine,
> but a crushed spirit dries up the bones. (Proverbs 17.22)

> My son, pay attention to what I say;
> listen closely to my words.
> Do not let them out of your sight,
> keep them within your heart;
> for they are life to those who find them
> and health to a man's whole body. (Proverbs 4.20–2)

> Do not be wise in your own eyes;
> fear the Lord and shun evil.
> This will bring health to your body
> and nourishment to your bones. (Proverbs 3.7–8)

It seems, then, that although our beliefs, notions and convictions have all resulted from our experiences, including our formal education, these in turn affect our behaviour, dictate our attitudes and to a greater or lesser degree impinge upon our emotions and our bodily health. St Paul, writing to the Philippians, says: 'Finally, brothers, whatever is true, whatever is noble, whatever is right, whatever is pure, whatever is lovely, whatever is admirable – if anything is excellent or praiseworthy – think about such things' (Philippians 4.8).

How do we feel? How do we respond?

Only the individual really knows how s/he 'feels'. Other people may assess how we feel from our behaviour, but of course we know that they may get this assessment sadly wrong. We can, of course, *tell* people how we feel. Above I have used the word 'respond'. Respond to what? I am thinking here of how one person responds to another, or how a group responds to another group, or even how a whole nation responds to another nation. I am going to look at human interaction here, for few would disagree with the statement that these two aspects of human behaviour, feeling and responding, go together: 'Oh, do forgive me, I didn't mean what I said, I was in a bad mood'. What is a 'bad mood' if it is not about feelings? And, clearly, before this plea for forgiveness, there had been some interaction!

So far I have used the word 'feelings' and have spoken of how one 'feels'. But because I am interested mainly in human psychology and spiritual life, I need to define a little more clearly what I mean when I use these terms in the present discussion. For example, it is a very different idea we have in mind when we say 'I feel cold' to when we say 'I feel angry'. In the first example we are referring primarily to a physical experience, but in the second we are referring to an emotional one. Psychologists might use the term 'affective' where I have used the word 'emotional', but readers will be clear about what we mean by 'feelings'. We are using the word to refer to emotional (affective) states such as joy, sadness, anger, jealousy, disappointment, and so on.

In previous chapters I have given many examples of feelings, and of the interaction that results from, or is in other ways connected to, these feelings. The Bible is full of accounts with similar links between feelings and interaction, feelings and behaviour. Even as early as Genesis 4 we have the story of Cain and Abel: 'So Cain was very angry, and his face was downcast . . . And while they were in the field, Cain attacked his brother Abel and killed him' (Genesis 4.5, 8).

All good stories and plays are about human interaction and feelings. They may have other elements, such as human endeavour, but without interaction and the emotional content they would be bereft. Some of the most poignant stories are told in the Bible. Think of the young woman who was dragged before Christ and accused of adultery. There followed interaction not only between her and Christ, but also between Christ and the accusers. Why did the accusers slowly, quietly, creep away one by one? What did they *feel* when Christ asked that the one without sin in his life should throw the first stone? Each felt guilty of something; each reacted by creeping away – feeling and responding.

I shall consider a few of the cases presented in the previous chapters and look again at the feelings, and the behaviour associated with those feelings. But before doing so, there are two more words that I have to use when discussing behaviour and emotions. The first word is *attitude* or *attitudes*. This is an important word because all of us have developed attitudes about things, people, ideas, religions, politicians, doctors, clergy, behaviour, children – and almost everything else we can think of. Attitudes involve feelings.

The other word is *prejudice*. This word means that as soon as we hear, see or talk about a subject we 'jump to a conclusion', or we 'paint them all with the same brush'. In fact, as the word indicates, we pre-judge: 'All politicians are liars', 'I wouldn't trust a gypsy any more than I'd trust an estate agent'. We can see that this word is also linked with 'attitude' and with 'feelings' and 'interaction'. Wonderful how they all link in together!

Social psychologists make a special study of such behaviour as prejudice, bias and attitude. They are able to tell us how these behaviours or ideas affect not only individuals but also groups of people. For example, it is interesting to see what happens when a larger group of, say, office workers is divided randomly into groups of three and given one room each. Let's say there is only one 'kitchen' available for all three groups. Sooner or later, complaints are received about the mess the kitchen is in, with unwashed utensils and the 'fridge door left open', etc. It might be discovered that the three groups must have come about by a 'remarkable coincidence' of selection because they are always able to point to one of the other groups, or both of them, as the offenders. Their own group 'would not do things like that'. This group loyalty tends to develop whenever people have been together for a time, and 'outsiders' become seen as threatening or 'different', but along with group loyalty come prejudice and bias towards other groups.

There are many examples of prejudiced attitudes in the Bible, quite apart from the intense prejudice shown to Jesus. Consider this passage from John's Gospel: '"Nazareth! Can anything good come from there?" Nathanael asked' (John 1.46). Nathanael seems to have been buttonholed by Philip who was agog with having found (or been found by) 'Jesus of Nazareth'. He said, 'We have found the one Moses wrote about in the Law, and about whom the prophets also wrote . . .' In modern, colloquial English, Nathanael's reply was something like, 'Don't be ridiculous, he can't be anything special or good – he comes from *Nazareth*.'

So how did the people in the case histories in this book feel, how did they respond, how did they interact, and did they display prejudice? Fear lurked behind many of the experiences people brought to the therapy sessions; feeling afraid was often an issue. Yet fear did not always have the same quality. More often than not it was an element of anxiety. There were people who were afraid they might do something in an uncontrollable way. They suffered from obsessional compulsive phobias. There was Marilyn in Chapter Three who experienced awful irrational fears about stabbing her own children. There was a different kind of fear referred to when I discussed Margaret's anorexic problems in Chapter Two. This was the fear that some adolescent and pre-puberty children experience concerning 'growing up'.

These are very differentiated experiences and come about as a result of a variety of external factors interacting with an enormous number of individual temperamental and personality factors. But along with these and other feelings went response. Some of the responding concerned the individual's own thinking about their fears, and some of it concerned the way they behaved towards other people.

Take, for example, Samantha, who we discussed in Chapter Four. She was a very anxious, unhappy Christian when she first discussed her problems – her 'presenting problems'. Because of how she felt, even after she had forgiven her previous husband for the way he had treated her and their children, she had a strong fear (an anxiety) that the Holy Spirit would abandon her. Her fear (we could say her 'thoughts') brought on the physical (skin) troubles of pruritis and urticaria. This irrational idea of being abandoned by the Holy Spirit caused her to respond to the children in a way she described as 'irritable and short-tempered'.

Now fear may be a proper response, a healthy response. Without the development of fear many lives would be lost. But this healthy, life-saving fear is generated by 'real-life' dangerous situations, and usually they don't last long. The disciples of Jesus were not being neurotic when they were frightened by the storm, although had they fully realized at that point just who Jesus was they would not have feared. They certainly, after Christ had risen, lost their fear of persecution, and many were prepared to die for their Lord. However, the sort of fear that harms us, the fear God does not want us to live with, is irrational fear that generates anxiety – anxiety that nags at us and pulls us down into depression or physical illness. We know it is God's will that we should be free of such negative anxiety from inner fear, because the Bible, in so many passages, makes this clear:

Cast all your anxiety on him because he cares for you.
(1 Peter 5.7)

So do not fear, for I am with you. (Isaiah 41.10)

Even though I walk through the valley of the shadow of
death, I will fear no evil, for you are with me; your rod
and your staff, they comfort me. (Psalm 23.4)

Clearly, the way we feel about events and the way we react and
interact are very real aspects of life. In previous chapters we
have seen that people have been affected by feeling 'trapped',
feeling 'hopeless', feeling 'guilty' or 'ashamed', feeling they
are to 'blame', feeling 'jealous', feeling 'left out', or feeling
'shy', and we could go on. Experiencing many of these feelings
is not necessarily bad or abnormal, and in real life there are
times when we *should* feel, whatever emotion it is. In fact, our
society has often been too keen to remove some 'feelings' such
as shame and guilt.

However, there are situations and conditions when certain
feelings are inappropriate and unrealistic, and there are some
occasions when the 'feeling', so called, is actually being
generated by physical illness. So we find the person who 'can't
stop crying' and who feels utterly depressed 'for no apparent
reason'. I have also mentioned the unrealistic guilt feelings of
those who have come safely through a tragic disaster. Often,
several negative feelings occur together or are experienced in
turn by a person suffering psychological pressure. In the case
of Ron and Sally (Chapter Two), you will remember the life
pressures that Sally experienced. Sometimes she felt 'trapped'
and at other times, or often at the same time, she felt crushed,
angry, jealous and suspicious. But she also felt 'terrified' of her
mother.

Sally was hemmed in by both Ron and her mother:
'Sometimes I feel trapped in life, like I must escape.' She also
said, 'I also feel that I've got to get people off my back. I want
to do my own thing and be *me* for a change.' Sally had a
mother who the outside world saw as a saint, always there to

help. In fact, Sally's mother had tied her daughter to herself, and in the early years had metaphorically bound and gagged her by a form of moral blackmail: 'What would your father have said?' Sally also suffered from what has been called the premenstrual syndrome, PMS for short. She then felt jealous, angry, suspicious, 'on edge', or sad at different moments. So here was a case where both counselling *and* medication were called for.

Sometimes 'feelings' that seem to go along with the person being 'ill' in some way appear to 'come from nowhere'. But 'nowhere', we find, may be some deep-down psychological factors or, for example, some normal change. Would one *always* judge it sinful to reject a child, one's own baby? The answer, the Christian answer, must be 'No – not always' – for consider the mother suffering with severe post-partum depression. In post-partum depression the mother, who at other times has proved herself to be a good, loving, caring mother to children already born and now toddlers or older, suddenly becomes depressed (or manic, or both) and turns against her new baby. She may have delusions and declare that the child is devil possessed, or is going to meet a terrible fate. She may have violent obsessional thoughts towards the child, or simply take no interest at all in the baby. There is little doubt that in the majority of these cases the condition is caused or aggravated by hormonal and other physical changes in the mother's body as a result of the recent birth.

We need to be very careful when judging a person's motives, or their behaviour. Of course, there is evil and sin, and we are all part of this, but we have to remember this passage: 'Why do you look at the speck of sawdust in your brother's eye and pay no attention to the plank in your own eye?' We need to keep in mind too that many people can be helped to develop new attitudes as a result of new insights concerning their own prejudices, fears, anger and motivation. They may also be helped by medication; often medication and counselling should go hand in hand, for both have potential for good under God's direction.

What pressures are we under? Where do they come from?

Consider carefully the following two accounts in which St Paul says something concerning himself:

> I have . . . been in prison more frequently, been flogged more severely . . . Five times I received from the Jews forty lashes minus one. Three times I was beaten with rods, once I was stoned, three times I was shipwrecked, I spent a night and a day in the open sea. (2 Corinthians 11.23–5)

> I do not understand what I do. For what I want to do I do not do, but what I hate I do. (Romans 7.15)

Both of these quotes are concerned with stress, and in some way with conflict, yet there is an essential difference. The quote from 2 Corinthians certainly conveys the pressure that Paul was under, the suffering, and sometimes the agony he bore. The quotation from Romans conveys the anguish he sometimes felt. Essentially, however, the first quotation concerns physical sufferings that came, so to speak, from outside of him, from others, and from external conflicts, while the second one is concerned with what we might call internal or inner pressures – to do with his own inner conflicts.

In various places throughout this book we have discussed situations in which people were experiencing stress, and often stress was associated with conflict. In our study of psychology and psychological experience these are important words, important concepts, and important experiences. You will notice that all these words and concepts are interrelated: they form a kind of conceptual network. Conflict and stress are clearly connected with anxiety and also with feelings, and in St Paul's case all these were associated with his beliefs. We study these aspects of human behaviour as if they were separate bits, but in fact they are all intertwined. Our account of Dave's problems (Chapter Four) brought out one example of conflict. He was only ten when referred for treatment. What were his conflicts?

Like every child, Dave wanted to be accepted by his dad. But his dad did not function on unconditional love, only conditional. Dave could have love if he was 'butch', 'macho', sporty and physical. But Dave was not made that way. He was poetic and artistic. So he was, to use a cliché, 'pulled in two directions', i.e. he experienced conflict. Conflict may produce stress, and stress may produce physical disorders. The stress young Dave was under caused him to stammer and to wet the bed – and these physical 'disgraces' simply increased the stress. He was not the only case I reported where conflict and physical illness were interconnected. There was also Jonathan (Chapter Three).

Jonathan, you will remember, was a very 'moral' man. He was honest, punctual, reliable and hard-working (conscientious in fact). His workmates, or many of them, urged him to be dishonest at work. They put him under pressure, perhaps unthinkingly, by telling him he should be behaving in a dishonest way. And of course Jonathan wanted to 'keep in' with them, to be accepted (as Dave did), but all the time he could 'hear' his mother's voice telling him to be upright and honest – conflict! There were other pressures, other conflicts and stresses, but the 'problem' Jonathan presented with was IBS, irritable bowel syndrome.

Then there was Bill, whose problems we discussed in Chapter Three. He was a social worker, a regional manager who could not control his temper. I mentioned that there were three ingredients in Bill's predicament, and that the first of these was stress. His experience of stress had increased with each promotional step. While discussing Bill's case I broadened our study a bit and looked at the way stress affects the immune system and other physical aspects, and I considered the effects of some tranquillizers and other drugs.

I also pointed out that 'stress' itself need not be harmful, and there is what I called 'good stress' and 'harmful stress'. Usually harmful stress is accompanied by some form of emotional conflict. This mixture is frequently found in matrimonial stress, and in other 'love' relationships. The adolescent Trixy in Chapter Four was loved by her zealous missionary parents, and she in turn loved them. But their very restrictive lifestyle – fine for themselves, but *imposed* upon their daughter – put Trixy under stress and introduced a conflict experience that she was unable to manage.

You may find it interesting to reflect on the 'internal' pressures concerning the people and their problems discussed above. With Dave (Chapter Four) there was the psycho-social pressure that came from his father. However, because of Dave's artistic temperament, this produced internal conflicts. In Jonathan's (Chapter Three) case he felt a strong internal conflict between 'being one of the boys' and his socially/spiritually developed moral inhibitions (perhaps between the *id* and the *superego*, to put it in psychoanalytic terms; or between the spirit and the flesh, if we put it in biblical terms).

Uncertainty

There is a thrilling little book by Bishop Roy Williamson entitled *Joyful Uncertainty*. Roy, as a bishop, first of Bradford and then the South London diocese of Southwark, decided to walk around his diocese, and this meant literally walking and hiking from parish to parish accompanied by groups of 'ordinary' folk from the different parishes and churches.

On these hikes Roy talked to teachers, farmers, police officers, accountants and many other workers. Naturally, the groups included parents, teenagers, people in wheelchairs – in fact, a lovely cross-section of citizens residing in Yorkshire and London. Nearly all these people, Roy says, were 'wrestling with inner contradictions' (Williamson, 1999).

He describes the pressure under which so many of these people live as Christians. He refers to a young secondary school teacher, Jean, whose faith is stretched to the limit. There was a time when she enjoyed taking assemblies, but at the time when Roy spoke to her she was 'terrified' about taking them. She experienced so much ridicule towards 'faith', and the secular influence was so strong that Jean really had to 'hang in there' as a believer.

The general message of Roy Williamson's book is that we may experience moments of doubt, or maybe just faith confusion, but it does not mean that we are at once rejected by God. But going further than this, the message from Roy is that we are not to despair or to be unnecessarily disturbed because some aspect of Christian belief (i.e. doctrine) is hard for us to accept. We must see our 'faith' as a journey, and as we proceed on the journey, holding to what we are able to hold to, a greater discernment, a greater understanding, will be experienced. If we are willing to keep on this journey, then through the work of the Holy Spirit we shall learn: 'And we, who with unveiled faces all reflect the Lord's glory, are being transformed into his likeness with ever-increasing glory which comes from the Lord, who is the Spirit' (2 Corinthians 3.18).

'That's fine,' some would say, 'but you are asking me to believe what I can't believe. I've been educated to know that there is absolutely no need to bring in the notion of God or a Holy Spirit to account for the existence of the universe. It's as if I were to say to you, "Just believe the moon is made of cheese". How easily would you be able to believe? You are asking me to be unreasoning and irrational!' This was one of the elements of life that troubled Bill (Chapter Three). 'Life's got no meaning now,' he said.

It is very important that we do not simply dismiss this sort of existential problem, for an aspect of human life is this quest for meaning. Another aspect is what we call 'rationality'. That word implies the use of reason. I would encourage any reader who feels that s/he must 'make sense of' our existence to pursue this study – if necessary for the whole of their lives. It will depend upon individuals as to how deep, how technical, how abstruse, a course of reading, debating, etc. they pursue, but they should know that it is no longer true that the debate is between scientists on one side and 'religious people' on the other. There are many thousands of scientists who are Christians, some of them 'top scientists'. There are many works written by physicists, chemists, mathematicians and others who are eminent in their own fields, but who also believe that 'faith' in God is rational.

One important caveat or proviso, however, if you *are* the kind of person who needs to explore the meaning of things. If you want to make a serious, in-depth study of the Bible, then try if possible to do this under the guidance of a Christian theologian who will put the Bible forward as an important guidance to truth. You may not agree on every point, but at least take the Bible study as seriously as you would take 'scientific works' dealing with the chemistry of life or a 'philosophical work' on the 'meaninglessness of meaning'.

I headed this section 'Uncertainty' and I have referred to faith. Some psychotherapists come across clients who are believers, but are apologetic – if not totally guilt-ridden – because, although they pray to God and are actually receiving pastoral help, they have to admit to uncertainty – a 'how can I be sure?' feeling. But does faith or trust have to imply certainty?

Certainty

It is easy to use words like 'certainty', and in everyday language people understand what such words mean, but if you get a group of linguists, philosophers and psychologists debating the meaning of these words, you would finish up, again, with uncertainty! So I shall keep to 'everyday language' in this section, and state that I am certain that the Bible contains promises and guidelines and warnings, which are important in terms of belief, trust and faith.

I am certain, for example, that there is a most wonderful, hope-generating message in the Bible that can be spelt out in this way: 'Because of God's love for us, each of us, we can be united with him. This is not on account of how *good* we are, but because a price has been paid and this was the price of the cross.' I am certain that such a promise is there in the Bible. A few quotations will prove the point:

> Christ suffered for you . . . He himself bore our sins in his body on the tree. (1 Peter 2.21, 24)

The blood of Jesus, his Son, purifies us from all sin. (1 John 1.7)

In him we have redemption through his blood, the forgiveness of sins. (Ephesians 1.7)

Look, the Lamb of God, who takes away the sin of the world. (John 1.29)

We can be certain, also, that the message that so helped Daniel, whose problems were outlined in Chapter Four, is there in the Bible. This message, you will recall, was about God's grace. Poor Daniel had an obsession about being damned. He had gleaned fragments of truth, but he had only grasped half the message. He had the first half, 'For the law was given through Moses', but not the second half: 'grace and truth came through Jesus Christ' (John 1.17). Read again how Daniel came to understand the parables of Jesus dealing with forgiveness. Believers can be certain that in the Bible there is a message that says nothing will be able to separate us from the love of God. And this message comes to us through the apostle Paul who was certain – he was 'convinced':

For I am convinced that neither death nor life, neither angels nor demons, neither the present nor the future, nor any powers, neither height nor depth, nor anything else in all creation, will be able to separate us from the love of God that is in Jesus Christ our Lord. (Romans 8.38–9)

These and many more such messages that are in the Bible give us reason for hope. This is not an irrational hope.

The Bible itself speaks of *faith*, which I have touched upon; it speaks of *hope*, mentioned above, and it speaks of the third in this trio, *love*. I shall return to the theme of love towards the end of this chapter.

Danger: unexploded bomb!

A notice with this wording used to be displayed in London during the Second World War to keep people from entering dangerous areas. To hear some well-meaning, earnest Christians warning others to have nothing to do with counselling or psychotherapy, one could be forgiven for concluding that they were talking of a danger akin to an unexploded bomb – 'Keep out, for your own safety; bombs can kill – so can therapy!' Of course, it is right to be careful, and even choosy, but could these people be behaving in an irrational manner, or even in a prejudiced way, in condemning counselling and psychotherapy? Such people, even some who are ordained, are afraid of psychology and any form of 'mind therapy'. We must remember, though, that a lot of fear and prejudice springs from ignorance. Sometimes people unquestioningly accept cartoon descriptions of therapists, or they condemn *all* of them because of what some unscrupulous ones do and think. We need to keep in mind a sentence written by the theologian Duncan Buchanan, the very first sentence of a book called *The Counselling of Jesus*. It begins with the words 'Jesus was the best psychiatrist who has ever lived.' There are people who argue that *any* form of mind therapy is dangerous because there are some forms that are bad, suspect, perhaps anti-religious and atheistic. Therefore, they say, play safe and have nothing to do with psychotherapy, psychiatry and counselling. Those who have this attitude are often being inconsistent and prejudiced. For example, they do not reject all forms of medical treatment just because the medical profession uses 'drugs', although 'drugs' have been responsible for a lot of unhappiness – the 'drug scene'. Nor do they reject all religious or theological ideas just because there are religious cults that are dangerous, and religious fanatics who are prepared to use themselves as human bombs.

Let us now look at the fears that some Christians still have concerning the mind therapies or so-called 'talk' therapies.

They would likely say that these were concerns rather than *fears*, but in reality it is quite likely that fear is involved.

Many Christians are troubled by what they think the philosophy or the beliefs held by the therapist may imply so far as treatment is concerned. For example, the question of beliefs in sin and evil. 'Is this counsellor or therapist going to attempt to crush such beliefs out of me?' they may say. First, you would have to have selected a very ill-trained and unprofessional therapist if s/he were a person who attempted to 'crush' any ideas out of you. But of course, as I have pointed out, people are free to select specifically Christian counsellors and psychotherapists. Even having said that, though, I would argue that well-trained secular therapists, or therapists holding other religious beliefs, would not attack their client's belief systems as such. You will have seen from some of the cases reported in this book that there are occasions, however, when well-meaning Christians need to have questions put to them, so that they themselves may reflect upon and pray about their understanding of Christian virtues, ethics, and even doctrine. Think of Daniel (Chapter Three) again, whose very concept of God was forcing him into depression. A Christian counsellor may help in this way. A *trained* secular therapist would leave this subject well alone, except possibly to assist the client to consider getting help from a Christian worker.

Some people may feel that the therapist is going to restructure their whole personality – 'I won't be me any more!' Anyone who has taken even a minimal amount of introductory training in counselling or psychotherapy would know that the idea of engineering some kind of personality restructuring goes wholly against the ethic and philosophy of modern counselling approaches. We know that there are various 'schools' of counselling and psychotherapy, but none of the accepted professional training bodies would qualify students who set out to manipulate in therapy. Even secular cognitive therapists, providing they are properly trained, avoid manipulation.

This should help readers to accept that the picture of the 'mind-bender therapist' is fiction. Of course, we all know that people can be 'changed' as a result of psychological pressure, and that there can be some very evil results. But this is more likely to happen in the so-called 'cults'. There is no doubt, either, that psychological pressure is used in advertising and political propaganda, to the extent that whole nations can change not only their beliefs, but also their treatment of individuals. Such a use of psychological knowledge and interactive social skills, however, would be anathema to any professional counsellor or psychotherapist. And while we are discussing change, it may be worthwhile to pause and to ask whether Christians especially should be rejecting the notion of change. After all, what is being 'born again' or 'conversion' about if it is not about change? Change itself may be helpful and desirable, but what people do not want is change that is forced upon them. Christ never forced anyone to accept a belief or to behave in a certain way.

Another fear some Christians have over psychotherapy concerns the beliefs and attitudes they feel the therapist may hold. Is he or she going to be someone who has a set of moral values and an ethical system based on post-modernism? Are they going to urge sex before marriage, wife swapping, 'expressing yourself' in every possible way – an attitude of anything will go? It is, as I have said, possible to find counsellors and psychotherapists who hold to Christian ethics because they are believers. But even they would not wish to impose upon their clients their own set of ethics – although if asked what they believed in they would be honest. If you look hard enough, you can always find those who are trying to impose their beliefs on others in any profession (sadly, even in the priesthood), but that is no reason to believe the whole of that profession is made up of people who spend their time converting clients or patients to their own belief systems. For what it is worth, most psychotherapists, even the 'purely secular' ones, make up a fairly conventional bunch of people.

There is, however, a distinction to be made between the goals of the Christian practitioner – who lets it be known that a spiritual element based on Christian belief and practice is part of the treatment offered – and the purely 'secular practitioner'. The secular practitioner aims to help the individual to accept himself/herself more, to change where change will help, and to become more contented in life. The Christian practitioner sees his/her goal as helping the troubled individual to grow into the freedom of children of God and his kingdom.

'Comforting words' and 'scary words'

There are some really lovely words in the now little-used Anglican *Book of Common Prayer* that always seem to touch me. Somewhere in the service for Holy Communion the priest says: 'Hear what *comforting* words our Saviour says . . .' etc. Then a bit further on: 'Hear also what St Paul says', and after each of these sentences some comforting texts are read out. (I've modernized the words slightly here and emphasized 'comforting'.)

Scattered throughout this book you will have noticed there have been texts – often 'isolated' texts – that were quoted to back up some aspect under discussion, and very often to show that comfort, spiritual comfort, is available in the Bible. Sometimes Christian writers may come under criticism for using texts in this way. There may be allegations of 'brainwashing', of 'mindless propaganda', or of texts being misused by being ripped out of context. I shall shortly return to these 'comforting' texts, but I intend first to briefly discuss certain aspects of the gospel message that are often ignored (and occasionally even denied) by Christians.

First, what *is* the gospel? What does the word 'gospel' mean? This word in English stands for a Greek (New Testament) word denoting the good news (tidings) of the kingdom of God and our salvation through Christ. But what does 'our salvation' mean? Here is a dictionary definition: 'deliverance from sin and its consequences and admission to heaven'. That is great news! So can I now just forget it and get on with life without actually having Christ in my life, 'in me'? The trouble is that people want the 'good news', naturally, but now they want to forget the other things that Jesus said. They want to forget altogether the text that haunted poor Daniel (Chapter Four): 'If anyone does not remain in me, he is like a branch that is thrown away and withers; such branches are picked up, and thrown into the fire and burned'. Christ did not mean that souls would be burnt in literal fire, but without his death on the cross all of us would be lost. We individually can still be lost – i.e. separation from God. That is worse than physical fire. However, the good news is that we *can* remain in communication with God. We have salvation through Christ's crucifixion, but we still need to accept Christ as our Saviour and follow him.

Speaking now as a psychotherapist, and leaving the 'scary words' to return to the 'comforting words', I would like to suggest that these words or texts, so stupidly ignored in much of our modern world, may – if used properly – have a remarkable psychological effect. It is easy to talk of brain-washing and the like, but psychologists know that states of mind (or 'states of brain') are important to mental health. We know, for example, that depressives typically have three negative perspectives. These are:

1   A negative interpretation of events.
2   A negative self-evaluation.
3   Negative expectations.

I call this the 'mind-set' of a depressive. There are, of course, various other mind-sets. What is important here, though, is to know that mind-sets may be altered. OK, this is not always easily done – sometimes psychotherapy or even medication may be required. However, a person's whole set of attitudes can be altered – that is, it is possible to change from a dysfunctional mind-set to a functional one. Most of the cases discussed in this book have illustrated such possibilities.

Taken as the basis for a new, uplifting, and positive outlook on life, the Bible as a whole (and the New Testament especially), if its teaching and philosophy is accepted, *taken in*, can become more effective than many drug treatment therapies. In psychological terms, it is possible for the subconscious *and* the unconscious to be positively affected by biblical matters. This 'bathing' in biblical teaching has been referred to in terms of 'training'. John Ortberg put it this way: 'Spiritual transformation is not a matter of trying harder, but of training wisely. This is what the apostle Paul means when he encourages his young protégé Timothy to "*train* yourself in godliness"' (Ortberg, 1997).

The formation of outlook and of attitude, or of positive and negative mental orientation, is something many of the modern 'cognitive' psychotherapies are interested in. These are psychotherapies that attempt to change outlook by what they call a 'cognitive' approach. Shields and Bredfeldt (2001), when they say that 'scripture teaches that our minds are the key linkage to our behaviour (As he thinketh in his heart, so is he, Prov. 23.7, KJV)', are discussing this cognitive approach.

So remember, the Bible used with prayer, and perhaps under the guidance of a pastoral adviser, can completely change outlook and feeling. Let's have one or two more 'comforters' before I go back to the 'scaries':

> Do not be anxious about anything, but in everything, by prayer and petition, with thanksgiving present your requests to God. And the peace of God, which transcends all understanding, will guard your hearts and your minds in Christ Jesus. (Philippians 4.6–7)

Note that the peace of God *transcends* (i.e. is beyond) all understanding – which means that all psychological 'explanations' fall short of the real power and effectiveness of the biblical messages. Another 'comforter' is: '"I am the bread of life," Jesus told them. "He who comes to me will never be hungry: he who believes in me will never be thirsty"' (John 6.35, GNB). Jesus talks here of spiritual hunger, and the 'bread' (the spiritual bread) is what we shall receive from being 'in Christ'.

Before we go on, I'd like to set you an interesting little search exercise! Take the 'mind-set trio' (the three negative perspectives on p. 164) for those who feel depressed, and search the Bible for antidotes to each of the negatives. I find it interesting, and rather strange, that there are some Christians who fear the effects of psychology on 'faith', and on the other hand there are others who do not seem happy with the term 'sin'. You will recall the discussion concerning sin following certain remarks Anne made (Chapter Two). There I discussed what are called 'sins of commission' and 'sins of omission'. So why do people, even believers, shy away from describing certain human actions as *sinful*? Often I find people equate such a word only with acts for which a person could go to prison – law-breakers of all kinds – and with especially heinous behaviour such as child abuse or murder. Sin is both much more than this, and – in human terms – much less. If you are a believer in a personal God – that is to say, a God who shows and experiences love, sadness, longing, anger and other 'feelings', magnified above human feelings by an infinite number, and who is perfect (in moral and ethical terms) – then anything we do that falls below this standard is sinful. 'Sinful' for me means 'outside God's character and his laws'. One of the great Christian Fathers, Augustine, said that, 'Sin is any word or deed or thought against the eternal law.' This last quotation I found in a useful book called *A New Dictionary of Christian Ethics* (Macquarrie and Childress, 2001), which I recommend to those wishing to delve deeper into these things. Moreover, I would say that the concept of 'sin' is not only compatible with the study of human psychology, but is *integral* to it.

Love

The bulk of this book comprises discussions concerning behaviour and emotions ranging from fear, through anger, and on to hate, yet I am going to close the book with a discussion on love. Why should this be? Am I simply trying to find a nice ending or trying to leave you with some nice thoughts? That may be the outcome, but it is not the reason for finishing with this theme of love. After all, the book is concerned with psychological health, mental health if you like, and the reason for finishing on this theme is because I believe love is fundamental to good psychological health, and I also believe God designed human beings so that they should have the propensity towards, and the fulfilment of, loving him: in other words, we were intended to be God-oriented and God-adoring. This being the case, any deviations from this pattern detract from the true psychological health of the individual, as indeed from the spiritual health both of individuals and of nations.

If this theme is expanded, we shall find ourselves examining several aspects of what I have, so far, loosely termed 'love'. For example, I shall look again at attachment, which we discussed in Chapter One. Attachment concerns the developing relationship between child and parent or parent substitute, and also between siblings. The scientific study of attachment has been a purely secular study, but part of my thesis states that the purely secular and scientific studies of human beings reflect again and again so much of what will ultimately be recognized as spiritual and metaphysical. I can say this even though, as a psychotherapist, I am well aware of the basic physical factors in mental health – including brain chemistry, neurophysiology, molecular biology and even elementary particle physics.

It is extraordinary how certain ideas are taken up in the popular media and received by the masses and then stick around for years becoming almost folklore. Some of these ideas were allegedly based on 'scientific' study, but an unbiased examination of the facts would reveal that the methods used (i.e. methodology) were flawed and the conclusions reached relate more to the preconceived ideas held by the 'scientist' than to scientific evidence itself. Sometimes, which is more extraordinary, the professionals accept these ideas and then the public just receives them, second-hand, without fully understanding them. One such idea, put forward as the result of 'scientific' practice and the 'enlightenment' coming from psychoanalysis, is Sigmund Freud's idea as to how human beings came to believe in God. In many ways, Freud was a genius and led the way in much of our thinking about human behaviour, but any unprejudiced psychologist or psychoanalyst today would agree that some of his ideas do not really stand up to scientific scrutiny.

Freud believed, and this of course fitted neatly into his own general atheistic beliefs, that the idea of God is only a delusion, but one that served a psychological purpose. He felt, and this would be consistent with Victorian and mid-European ideas of fatherhood, that the father played the important part in early childhood of setting moral and ethical standards and being the representative of moral authority. As the child grows up, the role of the father is carried on by teachers and others in authority. All these influences cause the child to develop a conscience about 'good' and 'bad' and also produce a continuing need for a higher authority figure – God. The individual, because of the 'father complex', is left with this longing for a father figure and, because of this, over the course of history humankind developed the idea of gods and, later, one God.

If you actually read Freud's texts all this rather simplistic and poetic material sounds extremely profound and deep and scientific. We find also discussions on 'ego ideal' and 'superego' (what we have loosely termed 'conscience') and references to the Oedipus complex, and so forth. But in fact this explanation for the idea of God is no more than a personal hypothesis that is consistent with much of Freud's 'scientific' explanation of human psychology, and therefore is an attempt at a rational explanation. I don't pretend that a 'scientific approach' can prove or disprove the existence of God, but I do believe that faith is rational.

But what about Freud's most famous students, those who at first went along with his ideas? Some of the most eminent, such as Erik Erikson, Alfred Adler and Carl Jung, eventually moved away from much of Freud's teaching (not that a Christian therapist would accept all of their teachings either). Carl Jung, while wishing to keep his psychoanalytical work as a separate medical entity, did in his own private life indicate that he had very different views about God than Freud did.

An oft-quoted statement by Carl Jung is the one he made in 1961 shortly before his death when interviewed by John Freeman of the BBC. John Freeman asked Jung if he believed in God, to which he replied, 'I don't need to believe, I know' (of God's existence). But Jung also noticed that even in his time there was a sickness among people, many of them well educated – but all of them showing signs of dissatisfaction with secularism and what they understood as rationalism: 'Among all my patients', he wrote, 'in the second half of life – that is over thirty-five – there has not been one whose problem in the last resort was not that of finding a religious outlook on life. It is safe to say that every one of them fell ill because he had lost what the living religions of every age give to their followers . . .' (Jung, 1958).

Another of Jung's observations, incorporated into his treatment approach, resulted in his seeing the individual man and woman as incomplete, as psychologically unfinished, and as needing (especially in the second half of life) to reach a higher and more satisfying realization of who and what they are, physically, socially and spiritually. To, in fact, 'acknowledge and live out his or her own essential truth' (Bryant, 1983, p. 89). Now this is a seemingly difficult process to understand, and I do not need to discuss it much further except to say that Jung called the process *individuation*.

But what does all this remind us of? Isn't this complex psychological process something that in any case would be involved in a process spoken of in the Bible and open to all people? Isn't the very best form of 'individuation' the process of being 'born again in Jesus Christ'? Individuation is said to be an ongoing process; the individual receives new insights and lives are changed. But being 'born again in Jesus Christ' also implies just a beginning, from where the individual then progresses spiritually.

It is interesting to note that other, more modern, schools of psychology also incorporate this idea of the need to develop psychologically to something nearer to the ideal. If we take Abraham Maslow's so-called 'humanistic psychology' approach, for example, we find that the individual has to 'satisfy' a number of needs as s/he progresses through life, but to become a more fulfilled individual there is finally the drive to *self-actualization*. Likewise, if we take the so-called 'client-centred' approach of Carl Rogers we find him writing of the *actualizing* tendency: an innate tendency in human beings to develop to the fullest possible potential.

If these needs, tendencies and drives towards fulfilment are recognized by the secular psychologies, does it not seem that what Christians have been talking about for millennia is really what the psychologies are all missing? Rather than an invented God of Freud, does it not begin to look as though all humans are made that way – reaching out for something higher, for God, because they are in fact, as the Bible teaches, beings made in the image of God. Of course, this is a matter of faith, but it would appear that there are more indications in modern psychology that human beings have an innate need for spiritual fulfilment than ever there were in the Freudian explanation of 'father seeking'. Human beings are homonomic. What does this mean? It comes from the word 'homonomy', which means 'in union with a greater whole'. That is the way we are made; God intended us to be homonomic in the sense of being in union with him, but sin separated us. Nevertheless, the innate need for full homonomy is there. The innate need to be united with God is there. Moreover, we see this human need, to be united with God, reflected in human psychology, and in the human psyche.

All that has been written about the importance of the attachment process reflects this need and tendency. Even the so-called 'New Age' search for contact with cosmic energy or a Higher Being reflects this homonomic factor. We were meant to be with God; we were created to be with God. The history of humankind is the history of anthropological homonomy. Yes, of course it is a matter of choice whether one accepts this explanation, or Freud's, or any other explanation for our tendency towards religion, towards union with God. But if we have faith in God through Christ, it makes sense, it is rational. To see ourselves as created with a natural leaning towards God, and a longing for closeness to him, be it conscious or unconscious, is rational, it 'makes sense'.

In Chapter One I expressed the desire that this book might prove to be 'a journey of discovery'. I also pointed out that with the God-given entities of love and attachment, much could go wrong; likewise, at the start of our journey we saw (along with Shields and Bredfeldt, 2001) that:

- Humans are divine image-bearers.
- Humans are both physical and spiritual.

Because of our physical and spiritual nature there is a need, in times of illness or emotional stress, for us to be treated in a holistic way. The whole person – physical, psychological, social and spiritual – calls for help. My hope is that this book may have helped some readers to accept that counselling and psychotherapy have a part to play in this, along with drug therapy, surgical and pastoral care.

> Hear what comforting words our Saviour says to all who truly turn to him: 'Come to me, all you who are weary and burdened, and I will give you rest.' (Matthew 11.28)

Appendix A: Psychotherapy and Counselling Organizations

National bodies/organizations for psychotherapy (these will put people in touch with trained local therapists):

United Kingdom Council for Psychotherapy,
167–169 Great Portland Street,
London W1W 5PF.
Tel. 020 7436 3002
e-mail: ukcp@psychotherapy.org.uk
Website: www.psychotherapy.org.uk

The British Confederation of Psychotherapists,
37 Mapesbury Road,
London NW2 4HJ.
Tel. 020 8830 5173
e-mail: mail@bcp.org.uk
Website: www.bcp.org.uk

National bodies/organizations for counselling (these will put people in touch with trained local counsellors):

The Association of Christian Counsellors,
29 Momus Boulevard,
Coventry CV2 5NA.
Tel. 0845 124 9569/9570
e-mail: office@acc-uk.org
Website: acc-uk.org

The British Association for Counselling and Psychotherapy,
1 Regent Place,
Rugby,
Warwickshire CV21 2PJ.
Tel. 0870 443 5252
e-mail: bacp@bacp.co.uk
Website: www.bacp.co.uk

Appendix B: Christian Counselling/
Counsellors

In selecting a specifically Christian counsellor or an organization offering Christian or spiritual counselling, it is advisable to be as careful in selection as when considering any other type of therapist. A major problem is that it has become fashionable for people to take short courses in 'counselling'. Some of these are *very* short – a matter of only a few days; others may run for several months. But often the person who has 'trained' in this way is in fact badly trained, because they have had only a smattering of counsellor training. Another problem is that some churches are sending their own members on courses and encouraging them to counsel other members of the same church or congregation. This is not necessarily wise or helpful, and much depends on what is meant by 'counselling'.

People often quote 1 Thessalonians 5.14 as an injunction for general 'counselling' of one another, or Ephesians 4.11–12, where it is pointed out that various people in the church – ordinary people – are given gifts such as evangelizing, teaching and pastoral caring. However, although there is an argument for saying that these passages refer to such aspects as listening, supporting, comforting and advising – and even supervising as a pastor – it is clear from closer study that what is meant nowadays by counselling, and especially professional counselling, is not what is implied in these Bible texts.

It is fine for groups of believers to comfort, advise, listen and support. This indeed is what should be happening. But readers will understand from the cases referred to in this book that attempting to deal with phobias, depression, panic attacks and even free-floating anxiety other than by prayer and friendly support, could very well lead to increased problems. Unless the person offering counselling, of the sort I refer to here, is well trained and holds a qualification in counselling, dealing in depth with these psychological conditions is not advisable.

Professional counsellors and psychotherapists do not offer treatment to their friends or family members, nor, if they are churchgoers, is it wise to attempt to become the therapist to the congregation (although there may be *occasional* special cases where this is acceptable). To help people who really suffer from the sort of problems discussed in this book it is often necessary for those seeking help to reveal secrets about their lives and thoughts that would, if they were regularly meeting the therapist in other settings, be quite embarrassing and uncomfortable.

So, be careful. Make use of the organizations listed in Appendix A, and remember that, as the writer in *A Time to Heal* says, 'Claims that the Holy Spirit will guide those with a spiritual gift for counselling need to be tested with care' (House of Bishops, 2000, p. 113).

References

Ashton, M. (1987) *A Mind at Ease*. Overcomer Publications, Poole, Dorset.

Barclay, W. (1975) *The Daily Study* (Matthew), vol. 2, chapters 11–28 commentary. St Andrew Press, Edinburgh.

Bowlby, J. (1986) 'The making and breaking of affectional bonds', in *Working with Children*. Tavistock, London.

Bryant, C. (1983) *Jung and the Christian Way*. Darton, Longman & Todd, London.

Buchanan, D. (1985) *The Counselling of Jesus*. Hodder & Stoughton, London.

Collins, G. R. (1989) *Christian Counselling*. Word Publishing (UK) Ltd.

Dalton, K. (1990) 'Premenstrual syndrome and postnatal depression', in *Health and Hygiene*, no. 11. Royal Institute of Public Health and Hygiene, London.

Davies, G. (1988) *Stress, the Challenge to Christian Caring*. Kingsway Publications, Eastbourne.

Deurzen-Smith, E. van (1988) *Existential Counselling in Practice*. Sage Publications, London.

Dickens, C. (1836) *Sketches by Boz*.

Duncan, D. (1981) *Love, the Word that Heals: Reflections on 1 Corinthians*, chapter 13. Arthur James, Hampshire.

Fahlberg, V. (1991) *A Child's Journey Through Placement*. British Agencies for Adoption and Fostering, London.

Frankl, V. (1973) *The Doctor and the Soul*. Pelican, London.

Hayes, N. and Orrell, S. (1987) *Psychology – an Introduction*. Longman, London.

House of Bishops (2000) Church of England Review, *A Time to Heal*. Church House Publishing, London.

Jung, C. (1958) *Collected Works*, vol. 11, para. 509. Routledge & Kegan Paul, London.

Katz, M. (1997) *On Playing a Poor Hand Well*. W. W. Norton, New York.

Kovel, J. (1986) *A Complete Guide to Therapy*. Penguin, Harmondsworth.

Lockley, J. (1991) *A Practical Workbook for the Depressed Christian*. Word Publishing (UK) Ltd.

Macquarrie, J., and Childress, J., eds (2001) *A New Dictionary of Christian Ethics*. SCM Press, London.

Maine, M. (1993) *Father Hunger*. Simon & Schuster, London.

Marshall, E., and Hample, S. (1967) *Children's Letters to God*. Collins, London.

Mathews, C. A. (1990) *Breaking Through*. Albatross Books.

Ortberg, J. (1997) *The Life You've Always Wanted*. Zondervan, Grand Rapids.

Parker, R. (1993) *Forgiveness is Healing*. Daybreak, London.

Rapoport, J. (1990) *The Boy Who Couldn't Stop Washing*. HarperCollins, London.

Rowe, D. (1991) *Breaking the Bonds*. Fontana, London.

Schaffer, U. (1983) *Greater Than Our Hearts*. Hodder & Stoughton, London.

Sherrer, Q. (1997) *Miracles Happen When You Pray*. Zondervan, Grand Rapids.

Shields, H., and Bredfeldt, G. (2001) *Caring for Souls*. Moody.

Simpson, R. I. D. (1992) *Understanding PMS and Its Treatment*. National Association for Premenstrual Syndrome, UK.

Todorov, T. (2000) *Facing the Extreme.* Phoenix, London.

Tournier, P. (1983) *A Doctor's Casebook in the Light of the Bible.* SCM Press, London.

Townsend, A. (1990) *Faith Without Pretending.* Hodder & Stoughton, London.

Tweedie, J. (1993) *Eating Children.* Viking, London.

Vine, W. E. (1985) *Expository Dictionary of Bible Words.* Marshall, Morgan & Scott, London.

Waskett, C. (1993) *Counselling People in Distress.* British Association for Counselling, UK.

West, W. (2000) *Psychiatry and Spirituality.* Sage Publications, London.

White, J. (1982) *The Masks of Melancholy.* Inter-Varsity Press, Leicester.

Wilkinson, H. (1984) *Puppet on a String.* Hodder & Stoughton, London.

Williams, R. (1999) *Joyful Uncertainty.* SPCK, London.

Winbolt, B. and Tyrrell, I., eds (1993) 'Confronting the Fear' in *The Therapist.* Spring, no.1, vol. 1. Human Givens Publishing, Chalvington, UK.

Yancey, P. (1997) *What's So Amazing About Grace?* Zondervan, Grand Rapids.

Young, J., ed. (2000) *Wrestling With Giants.* Hodder & Stoughton, London.